Phoenix Bound

An Adoptive Mom of 13 Shares Her Struggle Raising Traumatized Children

Angie K. Elliston

The events of this book are true as they were documented and remembered. Names of people and places may have been changed to protect privacy.

Contact the author: Angie K Elliston
PhoenixBoundQuest@gmail.com
www.facebook.com/PhoenixBound13
www.phoenixboundbook.com

Book Cover Image designed by: David Mor

Forward

As an expert in international adoption medicine and child development for the past 30 years, reading "Phoenix Bound" brings home the complexities that adopted parents are challenged with in dealing with children coming from traumatic backgrounds. While this book not only highlights the intense struggles of the children as well as the adopted parents who are often left with virtually no substantial support from educational, psychological or private sectors within the community, the book also brings forward the innate strength and resiliency of families such as this one who have taken upon themselves to "navigate the maze" of unchartered and "restricted ground" as our educational, psychological and social service system has absolutely and unequivocally no "unified understanding" of how to deal with adoption-trauma cases in children who have come from the most profoundly damaged backgrounds.

Additionally, the authors of this book have found their own means of developing a "support system" and, painstakingly, have found a way to develop a "set of resources" with adoption medicine professionals who have been able to both support them while also unraveling the mysteries and complexities that all of their children have been challenged with throughout the course of their development.

Phoenix Bound makes no secret of the severity of abuse, neglect, deprivation, chaos and confusion that their children have experienced in their home countries in addition to the unwillingness of American medicine and psychological professionals to understand and support their cause. This is an incredible book highlighting the resiliency of the human spirit of the children in addition to the incredible commitment of parents who have taken on the most damaged children in which traditional psychology would have failed them every time and the parents, themselves along with their own "network" have found ways for positive change and rehabilitation on their "Phoenix Bound Quest."

It is with great pleasure and respect that this forward is being written as this book will provide a "road map and blueprint" for other families who continue to be on a journey in finding ways to find peace for their children as this family has found in the warmth of Phoenix as well as the community which has welcomed the entire family.

It is truly a moving and poignant story that should be read by all adoptive parents and professionals alike who work with children and families from adoption-trauma backgrounds.

Dr. Ronald Steven Federici, Board-Certified Developmental Neuropsychologist, Father of Eight Internationally Adopted Children from Severely Traumatic Backgrounds.

Our children in order of oldest to youngest:

Kyle: *Had 2 siblings adopted by someone else before we adopted him. Adopted at age 16 as our third child.*

Drake: *Half sibling is Jadin. Drake was 10 when he was adopted by us.*

Miguel: *Half sibling is Jesslyn. Miguel was adopted by us at age 10. He had been in several foster homes and two adoptive homes prior to our home.*

Jesslyn: *Half sibling to Miguel who was never supposed to be adopted with Jesslyn due to their individual behavioral issues. She was adopted at age 10, a year after we had taken Miguel into our lives and adored him. She is the only child that looks like we could have given birth to her.*

Jadin: *Half sibling to Drake. Adopted at age 6.*

Brittani: *Sibling to Chloe and half sibling to Toni. Adopted at age 9 after feeling the rejection of several homes of relatives, as well as her foster home.*

Chloe: *Sibling to Brittani. Adopted at age 8 with Brittani.*

Tonita (Toni): *Half sibling to Brittani and Chloe. Adopted at age 8 after several years of weekend visits with us.*

Rebekka: *Re-adopted at 8 years old from her first adoptive home. Originally adopted from the continent of Africa at age 6.*

Josh: *Adopted from the continent of Africa at age 5-1/2.*

Anna: *Re-adopted at age 7 from the same adoptive home as Rebekka. Originally adopted from the continent of Africa at age 4.*

Samuel: *Adopted with his biological brother Josh, on his birthday, at age 3.*

Dawson: *Adopted at birth. Private adoption. We were chosen by the birth mother.*

(I use the word "adopted" here to represent the day they came into our home. In my heart, that is when they were truly adopted, as opposed to the day of their legal adoption.)

Reality Therapy

I often speak of Reality Therapy throughout this book. I have found that many professionals do not agree with this approach, but we have seen it proven over and over in the lives and struggles of our children. It helps with adults as well. We learned of it from Dr. Ronald S. Federici in Virginia, a neuropsychologist (an expert in his field) whom has been instrumental in our children's healing and successes. Reality Therapy can be used by ordinary parents like us. Reality Therapy is what the term implies. It is using reality to get through to a child. It is the ability to pull the child out of their destructive pattern and the reality they have created within themselves back into the reality around them.

Our children have twisted reality with their own attitude, belief system and anger. Reality Therapy is usually effective in setting their path a bit straighter. Sometimes they need several lengthy doses of Reality Therapy before seeing any change. With others' influences in our children's lives, we often needed to provide a great deal of reality.

Phoenix Bound

Anger and resentment rushes through my blood, but then, like a dam, forgiveness and pity stops it like a levy refusing to break. Arrests, deaths, fires, destruction, separation and blood haunt our tranquil dreams. It could have been much worse. It is not the life I envisioned when I began this adoption journey. So many things. So many memories. So many people hunting us down like hungry wolves scouring the land for their prey. I am lucky to have been wise enough to survive, but my husband was still in the land being hunted. I could only pray for safety, safety for us all in the end. So many hurtful, resentful thoughts of why we had to move. Why did it all have to end this way? Our hearts were of pure and noble purpose. We were not perfect, but we were not what we were being made out to be. Many have accused us of running from our peril and turmoil. We were not. We were running to something, something peaceful and conducive to healing. We knew we had to leave and leave fast. I drove away with not so much as a word to my husband, as if it was his fault I had to leave, but it was just as much my choice and our mutually-understood need. Soon, I prayed, he would follow.

With a lonely tear in my eye, I see our house in my rearview mirror - a beautiful house with elegant, stately Victorian architecture, renovated by my husband and me over the past fifteen years. I think I tried to force the displaced tear; after all, my life of unwarranted peril and fear deserved at least that much. Neighbors called our house "the house of the seven gables," a simple white house with burgundy shutters and door panels. Three chimneys decorated the majestic roof. A triangular window high in the attic gave the house a regal look. Directly below this unique window, down three stories, were the double doors with triangle panels and windows, which created a grand entrance to this grand house. The house was adorned with cherry bedroom doors and oak pocket doors leading into the formal parlor. We had added fancy window coverings

1

which gave the house the added touch of victory and sweetness. The deeply carved spiral wood work and polished brass door handles demonstrated the wealth and love the original owners had for this house. The fireplace stood with all its majesty with curves and designs in the center of the house, and ornate ceramic tiles served as a one-of-a-kind border.

Our house was originally the centerpiece of a special hillside property in a country setting, which in its regal past had been appropriately named Hillcrest. Hillcrest was originally a hops farm, funneling hops to a local brewery. The house included a servants' quarters in the back, for the hops workers and their families. These additional plainly-constructed four rooms added even more character to our unique home. The servants' quarters were of a simpler style, with shorter doorways, plainer woodwork around the doors and windows, and smaller rooms. This house was known as the most beautiful house in the area in the 1800's and early 1900's. We had planned to raise our children here, visit with our grandchildren here and stay here for the rest of our lives. We had no plans to move, but now we had to move to find freedom, peace and redemption for our family.

We gave away everything we ever owned or sold it cheap. Everything we had ever worked for and everything we had ever accumulated was now a memory. We had built up so much through the years. The most difficult things to get rid of were sentimental items: i.e. special gifts other people gave us like the stereo my brother bought me when I was in college; the antique couch I reupholstered for my mother for Christmas one year; and my sturdy canning shelf James surprised me with. My marble end tables were always admired and my custom-made extra-large book shelf I would surely miss. Shelves of board games had to be minimized to a few choice favorites and numerous bicycles, sleds and outdoor toys minimized to none. Our garage was filled with an air compressor, tools, extra wood, winter car tires, canning jars, outdoor toys and two sizes of ladders.

I remember my mother driving me by this grand house, one breezy fall day, pointing to it, saying emphatically, "I have found your house!" She and I had the same taste in houses. I teased her that she found my house, so she now had to pay for it. I showed my 28-year-old husband, and he agreed that it looked like an ideal home (once fixed up) for adopting several children, which had been my dream and purpose in life since I was a tiny eight-year-old skinny blonde girl. Little did we know.

My husband and I bought this nearly-condemned house on the same day the realtor showed it to us. It needed a new roof, a paint job, new porches, and a new septic. It needed someone to love it again, representing the shape our children would be in as they moved in with us. We had laboriously poured into this masterpiece, hours of back-breaking sweat equity, tearing down walls, sheet-rocking, puttying, scraping, painting and varnishing while dreaming of an adoption journey that would bring these children to a life of health and healing. We completed the finishing touches of our daughter Jesslyn's room at 3 am on a work night with the hope that she would feel at home when she arrived and less like she was a burden or displaced. Similarly, years later, I finished sponge painting Toni's room after the midnight hour bringing in the hope-filled New Year.

Our goal had been to help our adopted children feel welcome and have space to run and play. This was my dream home to fulfill that goal. My husband James had once declared we would keep this house into our old age, and I was not allowed to leave it for another. Now he is kicking me out. We cannot stay here. It is no longer our home; it is merely a house. I see it in my rearview mirror, but it is already a distant memory. I am not turning back, not ever. I know I will not, because I cannot. It is a shame. I cannot believe it has come to this. Why couldn't someone have had enough sense to stop it all? The social services system that should have been supporting us and protecting our vulnerable children led us to move and find peace. I am going to miss the down-home feel of country living, the tabs I could keep at the local fruit stand, hardware store and post office. I am going to miss the beautiful autumn leaves, warm breezes, winter sledding, summer gatherings at my parents' pool and dancing in the mud puddles. I will miss the good times. I especially enjoyed Mother's Day this past year on our wrap-around porch with my older children, grandchildren and our younger children grouped together for a photo, all stretching to be seen. But we are not leaving because of the good times.

My heart wanted to explode as I said goodbye to my husband of nearly 20 years. We did not know how long it would be until we would be in each other's arms again. In some ways, I feel as if we are still newlyweds, but we have been through so many challenges, it has begun to change us and age us. I think back at our youth - innocent, care-free, big dreams, and compassion filling those dreams. Dreams that, even though they were noble and good, would bring our lives to a critical cross point. I could now relate to indigenous people that are forced to leave their native lands they know and love. For many Native Americans, that journey has been penned the "Trail of Tears." Driving west with five anxious children and a one-year-old nervous Yellow Lab, we saw the sign commemorating this sad journey and I felt it. I felt an understanding. I felt the people's pain. I was one with their sad, lonely, scared, angry hearts of long ago.

Thirty Some Years Before

To get an accurate picture of how my family came to be separated by circumstance, and their home life uprooted by over a thousand miles, I will have to brief you on my childhood.

I remember making my life-changing decision and goal to adopt children at about eight years old. I could be a year or so off on my age as I was always tiny for my age; nonetheless, I can remember where I was. I was walking along the side of our barn where I learned how to ride a bike years earlier, thinking and praying. I felt that there were enough children in the world. I did not need to add to the population, but committed to taking care of the ones that were already born. I felt, at this young age, that there were too many children in the world who did not know that someone cared about them. I wanted them to know that someone cared about who they were and who they were to become. I never had the desire to have a child look like me or perpetuate my genes.

As a young teen, my parents decided to begin fostering children through the county social services in which they lived. They primarily took younger children as my mom enjoyed them at the baby stage best. I think this may have been a need she had after losing my baby brother at one month old from SIDS, a mysterious killer of baby's years ago (fortunately now SIDS is more understood and can often be prevented). Additionally, my mother originally wanted six children, but only had four biologically before my father put an end to the growing family. Her experience and relationship with the county social services system deterred me from any desire to be affiliated with foster care. I loved the children, but the uncaring, unprofessional, bureaucratic system was too much for my sensitive heart. I saw no good that a temporary insecure home did for these children who desperately needed security, love, and warmth. The children were treated like pawns in the chess game with four players: The County whom did not seem to have the child's interest in mind, the birth parents whom often held onto their parental rights long after they could logistically parent the child, the law guardian whom rarely knew the child before the court appearance, and the foster parents whom had no valid voice.

The death of a child is one of the hardest blows life can throw you, and my mother was left with a hole in her heart that needed to be filled. I think she found foster care to fill that gap and give her a sense of purpose in life. My baby brother's death was not spoken of much when I was younger, but I gathered information over the years based on comments and painful memories that played out in different ways. I learned that when we do not deal with our trauma effectively, it comes out in negative ways, affecting those closest to us. My mother's pain spilled over into our lives, but she persevered with strong resolution. I do know my mother always regretted not holding my baby brother one last time after he died in his crib. I learned this as I stood over my nine year-old adopted brother's lifeless body years later in the emergency room at the hospital. He had died as a result of getting hit by two cars while riding a bike with my Dad. My mother insisted I hold my little brother's hand. I grew up knowing that life is a part of death and the gates of heaven are wide open for babies, children, and believers, but to hold a dead person's hand was beyond anything I had ever done. It was not appealing to me, nor did it have any deep meaning to me at the time, but like a good daughter, I obeyed my mother. I knew it was something she wanted me to do and needed me to do. I trusted that she knew from experience what I would regret not doing later on in my life. She was right. I am glad I held his hand, and I am glad I held my mother's hand eleven years after that as she was struggling to take her last breath. But as a young teen, I had my mother in my life and learned of life and death mostly from raising pigs for meat, boarding an elderly race horse and simply being surrounded by more than twenty barn cats.

As a young teen, I had a big heart, full of compassion for animals and people. I babysat for a young couple struggling to make ends meet with seven young children. I never wanted more than what they could pay me, because I knew they needed a break from the demands of parenting so many young children and they did not have extra money to pay a babysitter. I stretched their dollar further by cleaning their house while they were away, even organizing their shoes. I saw it as an honor and a privilege rather than a chore. I fed on their amazement as they walked into a clean home and happy children excitedly telling their parents how much fun we had together the past few hours. My motto as a teen was that "I was here on earth to make other people's lives easier."

Before my parents took in foster children, they asked each of us kids our opinion. I essentially begged my parents to act on this decision as I had always written "baby sister" on the top of every preceding Christmas list. I loved children, and they loved me. However, I remember being disappointed when a homely, under-sized, unkempt, scraggly little girl was going to be my little sister. I did not want her, and I felt ashamed for feeling that way, especially based on outward appearance, but I could not help these feelings. Once cleaned up, I saw the absolute beauty in her shy, frightened eyes. Little Theresa and I became close even though she was two years old and I was sixteen. I took her under my wing and taught her, bought her clothes and toys, brought her places, and loved her more than anyone I had ever loved before. She was the baby sister I had always longed for. That young girl gave me a purpose in life and a drive to help children in foster care know that someone cared about them. I felt compelled to be the Dr. Martin Luther King Jr. of the social services system. I felt an innate need to educate, inform and reform surging up from my core. I recognized major flaws in a system – a system controlled by bureaucrats hell-bent on protecting their fiefdom. This system was ultimately hurting the same population it sought to protect: the children. Oddly enough, there is a telephone or internet survey for everything with the intent to be of better service to the public, but the social services system does not look for feedback and punishes those who offer feedback. My mother spoke up once and her home was put "on hold" without her knowledge, which meant that she was not able to get foster children placed with her, until a case worker informed her of it a year after the hold was put on. She had written a Thank You card to the Director of Family Services after her nine-year-old son's death, which included one line that caused this consequence: "Thank you for the beautiful flowers and card but Angie is my child too, and you are destroying her life and dreams." She rarely, if ever, advocated for me, as she lived in constant submission to the County, but I had never felt more honored as the day she showed me that card. Foster and adoptive parents alike live with an intense fear of losing their children if they think about speaking up against the social services system or advocating for a child in care. Why is feedback met with such offense, fear and anger? If feedback results in improving the services they provide and better care for the children in their care, why is it considered a bad thing? In the years to come, my file would become so large that one person could not possibly carry it, because they tracked everything I ever said or did in the community or regarding this system.

The little blonde-haired girl, who satisfied my greatest desire to have a baby sister, stayed with my parents for two short years before going home again to the same situation she had been removed from. From what we knew about her biological family's home, Theresa should not have been going 'home.'

At that time, I had gotten my driver's license and my own car. I cautiously called Theresa's birth mother and was fortunately provided with the opportunity to visit. I befriended the unstable mother and continued to visit her and her children until Theresa was put back into foster care, but this time in a different home. I was furious and deeply saddened that social services would put my little girl I loved dearly in a different foster home. I earnestly tried to visit and call her on the phone so she had some consistency in her life, but her new foster mother consistently lied and ignored me. She told me Theresa was not home, but as I heard the door shut and Theresa's voice in the background, the foster mother hung up on me. In the beginning, I was not allowed to see or speak with Theresa because "she was having difficulty adjusting to her new home." As I allowed time to pass and called her again, the foster mother refused to allow contact because "Theresa was well adjusted" and she did not want to jeopardize this. I tried to write to her, but the foster mother told me that the mail never got to her and the post office was unreliable. Each time I would get enough courage to call this foster mother or the County worker with yet another emotional plea, it ended with me crying buckets of tears for this little girl.

Thankfully, Theresa went back to her biological family, and I was able to resume visits. Years ago, I was angry Theresa was going back to the same situation she was pulled from, but now I was thrilled. When her foster mother told me she had gone home, I excitedly burst out, "Oh, good!" Confused, the foster mother began to engage me in conversation, but I hung up quickly, excited to resume contact with the little girl I fell so much in love with. Several years had passed so I had to re-introduce myself to this growing little girl. When I went to college, she again went into foster care and finally to a group home. I had such a love for this little girl; my heart ached when I was not allowed to see her. Amazingly, I was treated as if I was a bad influence (the one who had always tried to be there for her). I remember crying so hard I thought my heart would throb out of my chest. My main goal was to let Theresa know I did not forget or forsake her, but no one valued our bond. I continued through repeated heart wrenching disappointments to advocate for her and beg the County workers for some type of contact with her. At one point, I was allowed to take her for the day and spent hours collecting her siblings from different foster homes and then hours playing at the park, enjoying a picnic lunch. I was later accused by the director of social services of being "vain thinking that Theresa needed me." It is sad how little the County values relationships and bonding. I have to wonder if they have ever felt a closeness to anyone in their lives. Meanwhile, my educational goals were founded upon Theresa's disheartening situation. I was going to become a social worker. I wanted the children caught in the County's bureaucracy to know that someone loved them and cared about them.

In hindsight, I think I was so hurt because I was young and innocent – ignorant of the worldly, selfish ways of a bureaucratic system. I was also shy back then. As a result, the constant confrontations and turmoil with the County cut deep. I was trying to do everything I could, out of love, to help my former foster sister. I was not equipped to deal with how vicious, rude and uncaring the County workers were. I naively thought they were dedicated to helping foster children, while in reality control and power were their top priorities. (I do not believe in making overly broad generalizations, but in that situation I was put down, ridiculed and embarrassed. I was treated as if I had abused, neglected and mistreated a foster sister I had loved with all my heart.

A few years after Theresa came to us, while I was still living at home, a little bi-racial boy came into my mother's care at the young age of one and a half. He was a chunky beautiful little boy with big brown eyes and light brown skin. I fell in love immediately. This little 'chunker' stole my heart, but gave me a tongue. In my mother's care, he had little contact with his birth parents. His birth mother said she realized that she could not raise him and his two older sisters, so she chose to relinquish her rights assuming that the father would never get full custody. His father hung onto his parental right and seemed to have waited until the children were old enough to care for themselves. At age 10, visits with his father began and reuniting the family became the goal. It is said that one of the older girls had wanted to go home. She enjoyed the freedom of running the streets and doing as she pleased. This began a heartache that still hurts from time to time more than twenty years later. At the time of this writing, he is in his late twenties and is behind bars. My heart aches for him because he was not a bad child; he was a confused and angry child. He was powerless to a bureaucratic system that seemed heartless in its decision to send him to a birth father he did not know, did not trust and did not love.

He could not understand why the only family he ever knew was powerless, could not protect him, or stop what was happening to him. As a child, you naively believe that your parents can protect you from harm, but our family was as powerless as he was. This little boy and I wrote a letter to the State Commissioner, which received a great amount of attention at this time. In fact, I learned later that the letter was copied and sent to every caseworker in that County. Not surprisingly, this started my reputation with social services. The reputation led to much turmoil, conflict and angst over the years as I tried to raise our challenging family. The County viewed me through this lens for nearly 20 years. The years of conflict with the County at every turn eventually led to our decision to leave the County's oppressive atmosphere for more parent-friendly environs where we are free to raise our family as we choose.

I have learned that what my mother always told me was true. She always told me, "You cannot fight City Hall." Until recent years, I felt that justice would win. I thought that people would recognize injustice and stand up for what is right. Over 20 years later, I have seen the American people, in places of power and places of ordinary citizenship, sit back and for one reason or another, not respond to their responsibility of standing up for what was right, while poorly-educated, intemperate, obnoxious County workers attempted to inject themselves into our family life. The desire for justice and respect for liberty in America has dwindled.

Our Adoption Journey Began

James and I had met at my college job, working at a community residence for mentally disabled adults. He had just graduated from college as a finance major. I took an interest in him immediately and he enjoyed listening to my goals and dreams. We had known each other for little over a year and dated for 11 months, 5 of which were spent apart as James had signed up for military service, attending Basic Training and AIT. Six days after he came home, we eloped.

James and I were married outside in the winter with a minister, a photographer, and two witnesses in a gazebo with Christmas lights hanging beautifully. It was a quick and chilly wedding service. He spent the next nine years in the Army National Guard. I did not agree with his decision or enjoy him being away during our year of dating, but I respected him and honored his decision. Many people we knew joked that Basic Training would be easy for him after dating me. Others teased that he would find someone else while he was away and forget about me. I had no worries and enjoyed their fun at my expense. My only regret looking back is that I did not go to his Basic Training graduation. I felt that it would be too difficult emotionally to see him graduate and then be away from him for another three months of AIT. Ten years later, I made it a point to attend our son's Basic Training graduation, and I am glad I did.

I had only three marrying prerequisites: I wanted a pet pig in the house, to adopt several children, and to never live in Arizona. He agreed to each prerequisite. He was not sure about the pig in the house, but gave in to my persistence. Thankfully, it was a pot-bellied pig and only grew to about 60 pounds.

James and I had discussed adoption at length before we married, so once married we immediately began preparations to adopt. According to the County Social Services system, we had to take foster-adoptive classes. I do not remember learning anything new during the classes, but I do remember leading our own private joking section with every contradiction we heard. We were young and they were stupid. My parents had done foster care and adoption for years, and I was familiar with the inside story as I listened to their fluffy story of foster/adoption. They did touch upon the foster/adoptive child's inner struggles and the root of their behavioral problems, but they never had a solid plan of attack to curb these behaviors by reaching to the root cause. They seemed to fluff it by repeating their sympathy for the child and why he or she would be acting out. It tugged on our heartstrings, but never gave us any solid information.

It seemed like an eternity before the social workers completed our required adoption home study. Because we were focused on addressing the needs of the greater amounts of minority children waiting to be adopted, we needed to fill out pages and pages of ridiculous race-based questions, which essentially amounted to reverse discrimination. I called one of my best friend's fathers to whine about the injustice. Since he was African American, I was hoping that he would know the answers and have a great deal of sympathy for us. He was no help. He did agree that it was wrong and that it was reverse discrimination, but he would not show the amount of sympathy that I expected, nor did he answer the questions for me. He told me to read one question, get up from my seat, jump up and down, twirl around yelling, "this is stupid," sit down and write the answer. Then read the next question, get up, jump up and down, twirl around, yell "This is stupid!" sit back down, and write the answer and keep doing this until I finish all of the questions. I was inwardly furious at him for not giving me the answers to the questions in front of me, or at least helping me answer them, but I did what he told me to do and it worked. Sometimes, no matter how much we do not want to do something, we have to, to get where we would like to go and to get where God wants us to be. This was one of those times.

The day came when we were allowed to search for children in the Blue Books (pre-internet days). These Blue Books contained photo after photo of adoptive children and their siblings. I know for some, especially adult adoptees, this sounds inhumane and wrong, too much like "shopping" for a child. For me, it was a dream. I stared at these beautiful faces and prayed that someday each one of them would find a home that they could call their own and that someone would show them how much they were loved. I read nearly every description under each photo and envisioned them in my new family. I wanted all of them. I loved all of them. I felt compassion for all of them. However, realistically, I knew we were not ready for certain personalities, behavioral issues, and disabilities.

After months of (1) calling the Blue Book number for the number of the child's social worker, (2) then calling the appointed social worker for each child, and (3) then waiting for a return call, I began to realize that this method was a dead-end road.

To our surprise and confusion, the majority of the children in the Blue Books, were already placed for adoption, often with their foster parents. In other words, the majority of the children were not available. However, at the time this was the only way to search for waiting children. The internet was non-existent and we were not allowed to randomly ask social workers if they had any waiting children on their list for a family such as ours.

Long-distance call after long-distance call came up void, became expensive, and time consuming. My heart sank, and I began to wonder if there were any children in the country waiting to be adopted even though every commercial and written article declared that more than 100,000 children were waiting for adoption. We had no preferences except that we wanted hard-to-place older children, which to us seemed like it would have been easier. We had no preference of gender, age, ethnicity, race, or number in the sibling group. I was secretly praying that we would find a sibling group of ten that no one else was prepared to take or felt they could handle. We could keep the sibling group together, so they could not only know each other, but grow up with each other.

Eventually, our case worker found two bi-racial boys, Jadin, age six and Drake, age ten, from another county. I was disappointed that it was only two boys, and in my heart was disappointed that the sibling group included a young little guy of only six years old. My heart was for older children, and I knew that other adoptive parents might have wanted a six year-old. However, since they seemed to be the only ones up for adoption in the United States, we accepted the pair, met them, and brought them into our family as our sons.

Predictably, we were naive to their needs, naive to their pain and loss, and naive to their potential behaviors. Regardless, we were excited and ready to take on the challenge of two young boys that needed a home to call their own. We knew little about them - their personalities, dispositions, or what their life was like before they found themselves living in the system. The social services system knows little about their children and often shares less than they know. Being moved between foster homes was familiar to them. We knew we had our work cut out for us, but we did not know the extent to which they would try to sabotage any good that we tried to build in our new family.

I began to notice the stress these two little innocent-looking boys were having on my body. During a walk around town, I would get so weak, I felt as if I would fall down in exhaustion. I got scared. I would see people pass me and want to ask them for a small bite to eat or a drink, but I was embarrassed at my weakness. Soon, I learned to bring my water bottle and quarters at the bottom of my water bottle holder for these situations. In an emergency, I could make a phone call or buy something small to eat with the quarters.

I also began to change on the outside. Throughout my life, my nickname had been Smilie. I smiled throughout life, most of the time, for no apparent reason. Smiling was second nature. I enjoyed life and the people in it. Within a short time of bringing these children into our home, my demeanor began to change. I was easily frustrated. I was lost as to how to reach these young boys. My smile faded and I was visibly miserable. James and I would spend hours at night after they were in bed, trying to weed through their behaviors in our minds, to find the root cause and address it appropriately. We were tired and worn out. Every approach was met with more disobedience, disrespect and frightening behaviors.

Others were noticing that despite realizing a lifelong dream I was becoming miserable. I began to cuss at home. I had never sworn before the age of 26, but I began to swear. I thought swearing would show them how serious we were. I learned the hard way that evil does not fight evil. I quickly regretted compromising what I strongly believed in. The areas that we compromise in our life stay with us until we weaken enough to hand it all over to God and allow Him to transform our heart. Until then, it remains a part of us.

Being young, I had thought that if you live right and make good choices throughout life, you would be rewarded and things would go well with you. I guess at the core of it, I thought if I was good enough, I would not have problems. For example, I had made the noble decision to adopt older troubled children, life would then go as planned. We would get through to their troubled spirits and 'fix' them and we would all live happily ever after. I have since learned that this is not true. You cannot 'fix' people without their permission and will, and sometimes life just is not fair.

Their behaviors were constant and deviant. We had no one to talk to. We could not share these behaviors with friends because they were often sexual in nature or simply not socially acceptable. We were embarrassed that our children were sexually acting out and had no idea where to turn. The boys were unexpectedly unresponsive to consequences and discipline. Nothing we were experiencing was spoken of in our foster-adoptive classes. One class had us check off the behaviors James and I would not be able to handle, and I remember clearly checking off lying. Lying, for Drake and Jadin, were survival behaviors and were used daily. We were drowning in these unexpected situations and lack of help. I turned to talk radio. The Dr. Laura Schlessinger talk show emphasized doing the right thing even when it is hard. The kids and I would listen to her radio show and talk about it. I attempted to think outside the box and reach the root of their behaviors. I knew they had adoptive issues that I did not understand, and so I introduced them to adult adoptees and had them write to them with adoption questions. I also took the time to research on their behalf.

We tried to teach, preach, logic, lecture, spank, give out consequences or punishments, and encourage our boys. None of these had any effect, except perhaps to increase the behaviors. Fire starting, sexual deviance, lying, deceit, sneakiness, manipulation, stealing, abusing our animals, urinating and defecating in unwanted places became our family life. We also sat them down to explain the crossroads in their lives and where each road would lead. We were blunt and to the point. All of this occurred while the boys looked compliant and innocent in public.

Their brains seemed to fixate in one direction, making it impossible for them to turn their behavior around. It was as if their brains could not look for different ways of doing things or different solutions to any given problem or situation. In math, Jadin would refuse to write the number one while Drake would insist four times four was seventeen all day, no matter how many times he was corrected. They would both stare at their math or writing assignment for hours, even if we tried to help them. In sports, they would continue to make a mistake, without correcting it. For example, in basketball, Drake would continue to hit the rim of the basketball hoop rather than setting his feet differently, moving closer to the basket or throwing harder. In their lives, it would be difficult, too, to go a different direction in their brains. For example, when James and I had a fire drill in our home, James stood in front of the front door exclaiming that he represented fire. Both boys stood in silent confusion facing James. They had no idea what to do even when James told them they needed to find another way out of the house because he was fire. This became a huge frustration for us, as it crept into every part of their lives and our lives. Once again, we tried to teach this skill, to no avail.

Communication was no different. The youngest child, Jadin, held his emotions in and refused to communicate effectively when he was upset, which concerned me the most. I wondered how long a child could go, stuffing in his feelings and emotions, before he did something really horrible. He would exhibit behaviors rather than verbalizing his pain and confusion. Otherwise, we could not distinguish the older child's behavior from the younger child's behavior. We did not know it then, but Jadin had been told to admit to things he had not done by Drake. Jadin, being the shyer, younger child, obeyed his big brother. He would also act as the lookout when Drake was up to no good. We begged him to tell the truth and to talk to us when he was upset, sad or happy. When they were happy, they would impulsively do things without thinking about any types of consequences or right and wrong. When they were angry or upset, they would do impulsively dangerous things to feel better inside.

They both lied better than I had ever witnessed in my life. I am a country girl. Pure country, my word is my word. I was not accustomed to such lying, nor could I understand why someone would lie so much. We had given them a nice home with love and structure, sports, music, art lessons and travel. We strived to give our children many outlets for their anger, confusion and sadness, but these avenues did not seem to make any difference; if anything, it seemed to make the behaviors worse. To our surprise, on the morning of Disneyland, in California, the oldest boy, Drake urinated in his pants because he was not wearing the outfit he wanted to wear. On our trip home, he did the same thing in Dallas, Texas. He urinated in his pants in the car after we had stopped at a rest area only one exit ago, because I asked him to get into more comfortable traveling clothes. To a parent, it seemed to be logical requests. This type of behavior was constant and often not unexpected.

While James and I were watching TV at night, one of the boys snuck into our bedroom, started a fire and put it out in the middle of the bedroom carpet. While we were sleeping, one of them would sneak downstairs to the kitchen and play with the gas stove, charring the wooden cutting board with the open fire. It took us months to realize it was not every-day cooking that was causing those burn marks. Things would come up missing, smells would permeate the air from strange origins, things would mysteriously get broken, and things would appear that we did not own. Stale urine would be a background aroma billowing like smoke from our son's room. We were often confused, but we learned that when we "smelled fish, it was fish." In other words, when things did not add up, we knew something was amiss. We no longer trusted anything they said, but relied on our instincts and our five senses more. As things worsened, we tried harder to help the boys. We researched topics, reached out to firemen and policemen, begged older adoptees to share their success stories with our boys and looked for qualified adoptive counselors and pastors. We wanted so badly to help them become honest young men and positively contribute to the world and to feel like they had a family to remain in until they transitioned naturally at an older age. As time went on, our expectations lowered and we were hoping our boys would not end up behind bars. We wanted the best for them, and we felt that we could show them a positive lifestyle. We struggled mightily, but with each passing day, we felt like we were beginning to get through to them. James and I often talked into the night, brainstorming on how we could parent them better and what would make them feel more content and end the behaviors. Each new day, we worked to transform ourselves into parents that could successfully unify our new family. We were working with skilled sabotages, and my vision of motherhood was fading quickly.

Drake later admitted that he did these bad things to get moved to another home. He also told his group home worker that we tried to make him someone he was not. At first I was confused and disgusted. After all, we were not trying to make him a doctor, a lawyer or a priest. We did not force them to become Christians, but merely to try to uphold Christian ethics and morals while in our home. As I thought more carefully from an unbiased point of view, I understood him. I considered his comment from a deeper point of view and from the point of a ten-year-old maturity level. What we tried to change was to make him an honest, hardworking and moral guy. He did not want that. We also tried to make him fit into a family he was not ever ready to fit into, at least not the way we wanted him to. We were indeed trying to make him someone he was not.

To James and me, the unpardonable sin was sexual deviance and abuse. Now, I know that it is often a part of how traumatized children express themselves when stressed. I do not condone it and never will. It still crushes me, but I understand it. We have learned through the years, is to safeguard against this sexualized behavior, even if there are not any visible signs. Children fall back on what they are familiar with, what worked in the past to get removed from a placement, or what happened to them in the past. There are also more technological advances that would have helped us with our first two children. There are door alarms, driveway alarms, residential security cameras, baby monitors with cameras, and all sorts of advances that we were either ignorant to, or did not have available to us at that time.

Everyone Said NOT To Do It

James and I wanted to adopt a large family, but the adoption process was slow and tedious. One day, the case worker for our first two boys, whom we had befriended, called me at home. He explained that he had a boy on his caseload who'd announced his desire to be adopted and that we were his only hope. It was not necessarily that the boy was bad in any way, but he was much older than the typically sought-after adopted child.

I enjoyed being known as someone that could be counted on to handle a hopeless situation. In later years, we would continue to do this for people. To help matters, we had already met this boy. He lived in the same foster home that we adopted our first two boys from. He was described as an unmotivated 16 year-old who had not wanted to be adopted, but had changed his mind. He now wanted a family.

James and I each said, "Sure, why not." As we told people of our decision, everyone told us not to do it. They insisted that a sixteen year-old would be set in his ways and be impossible to change or mold into our family. Friends and relatives strongly advised us not to take him in to our family. Regardless of the warnings, we did not hesitate or doubt our decision.

We made arrangements to meet with him and take him out to a Chinese buffet to discuss the implications of adoption. We explained what it would be like in our home and what adoption would look like in our home. We talked and enjoyed dinner. In the end, this young man chose to come live with us. Kyle was now our son, taller than me, with dark hair that stood out to our blonde and red hairs, and a lean young figure. We both knew that Kyle may never see us as Mommy and Daddy, but he needed someone to lean on, talk to, and call on. We expected to be more like counselors and trustworthy adults throughout his life than a mommy and a daddy. His adoption day commemorated the anniversary of my major back operation for scoliosis ten years before. I chuckled to myself at life's twist and turns.

For years, Kyle would not say "Mom" as it was awkward to him. When he walked into a room to speak with me, he would clear his throat to speak and that was my cue that he was speaking to me. It worked for me and it worked for him. My name became, "Umm." I knew he needed James and me. He respected us for who we were and what we did for him. He still does, and all the more, as he now has a wife and three children.

My favorite story about Kyle is about the time he worked at a local factory along with his adoptive father and my brother. At lunch one day, one of his co-workers heard him say that my brother was his uncle. The co-worker was amazed as they were about the same age. Kyle got such a kick out of his reaction that he proudly pointed to James and said, "That's my Dad! And you should see my Mom!"

Kyle was not always easy, but he was never difficult. When he got too big for his britches and a bit disrespectful, we put all of his belongings on the front porch, and when he got home that day from work, we announced that he was moving out. In awe, he packed his belongings into the vehicle, and my husband took him to his new apartment. By then Kyle was nearly 18, graduated from our homeschooling, and held a steady job. It was not a high-paying job, but he could pay the rent. We visited him often and he visited us. He did fairly well in his apartment, but did not clean much. Through the next couple of years, he moved a couple of times and tried having a roommate.

At one point, I noticed he was depleting his savings awfully fast, so I made a beeline for the bank and withdrew the remainder of his money. When he asked me about it, I explained that I did not like what I saw and that I was worried about his choices. He admitted that he was going through his money quickly, but did not disclose what he was spending it on. I knew that he did not do drugs. He was always proud of that. He dabbled in alcohol, which I wish he had not especially given his background, but thankfully that ended when he experienced the beginning stages and symptoms of an ulcer. I had prayed for that.

At age 20, he came to visit to talk to James and me. He explained that the roommate idea was not working out and asked if he could live with us again. I immediately explained to him that he had to be respectful. We also asked that he pay a modest rent, more for his own good, to get used to paying a monthly fee of some sort. The plan was to use that money when he moved out for something that he would need.

He was extremely respectful. One day, he mumbled as I was dishing out dinner, and I abruptly turned to him, glared at him, and said plainly, "Do not even go there." He stopped mumbling immediately and showed respect. If he saw me sitting down with a book, he would seize the opportunity and talk endlessly at me. My job was to nod now and then.

Kyle was working full time at a local factory and doing well financially. He had built good relationships with nearby friends and relatives. In his heart, I think he felt like he was missing out on his biological family. We lived about 3 hours away from his biological brothers, sister, and relatives. He was emotionally close to his uncle that was around his age even though he was not always a good influence.

After several lengthy weekend visits with his biological family, he made the dreaded announcement that he was going back to live in the area where he grew up. James and I did not disagree with his decision, but he did not plan the move. Kyle wanted to leave right away. He quit his job with little notice and trusted his uncle to take over his truck payment and his four-wheeler payment. We feared the worst, and the worst happened. His four wheeler and his truck were repossessed and his poor financial choices still haunt him over ten years later.

He was able to reunite with his biological family, which included the good and the bad memories, the good and the hard feelings, and the good and the bad realities. He also found someone he wanted to spend the rest of his life with. He married her, accepted her child as his own, and has had two more children with her, giving us three of our grandchildren. He struggles with his upbringing at times. He has difficulty being attentive and nurturing because he never had that growing up. He struggles having the energy he needs for them when he is exhausted from work. He tries, and in so doing, he has conquered his past.

A Hurting Heart

Backing up a bit, to a year after we adopted Kyle, I continued to look for children to adopt. I was still looking for a large sibling group, but despite the statistics there were not any in the United States. There seemed to be a large brick wall separating prospective adoptive parents from the adoptable children in the U.S. After many phone calls, tears, prayers and questions, I found a case worker in the same county where the three boys came from who saw my plight. She was trying to find families for children on her case load.

One day I was on the phone with her and asked her a question about one of her boys. She misunderstood who I was talking about - we began talking about the other child of the two we both had in mind. It got confusing, so I stopped her and asked about Miguel. She made a quiet short giggle. I asked her, "What was that for?" and she replied that, "Every time I think of Miguel, I cannot help but smile. He makes me smile. I like him." That was it. I was sold. I wanted him. It might seem that James and I make these decisions lightly, as if getting a puppy, but we have continuously talked about adoption. It is our life's passion and we are committed to being ready at a moment's notice. We are prepared with the answer to the question before the question is asked.

I argued my case before James, and he agreed to adopt Miguel as our fourth child. We were aware of his behavioral issues, as well as his accusations against the foster/adoptive mother that led him to be removed from that home. We were leery. It is common for powerless foster and adoptive children to try to gain control over their circumstances by accusing innocent foster/adoptive parents of abuse.

Immediately, upon hearing that he was moving to an adoptive home, Miguel acted out in his temporary foster care home. For example, Miguel called 911 for no reason when he was on a school field trip to a science museum and his behaviors in his foster home became so bad, his foster mother was planning to have him moved. I spoke to the case worker in his county and said that I felt he was acting out because he was scared, and had a fear of the unknown. Rather than going slower with the adoption, I thought we ought to go quicker. That is in fact what social services normally does, pull children out of homes with no notice. Miguel had been taken out of several homes without prior notice or explanation. Miguel had notice of the placement with us, but it was too much notice and he was a fearful mess. This declaration caused friction between the two workers, his case worker and our county case worker. Our case worker told us, "Over my dead body, will you get your way. I disagree with you and it will go my way, not your way." We were upset because the unnecessary delay would ultimately hurt the child. Our worker's arrogance and mean tone of voice were shocking. Minutes later, he was eating his words and saying that Miguel would be dropped off the following weekend. The county case worker in Miguel's county agreed with our strategy.

We had won a small, but important victory. It felt good to get our way because we were convinced that Miguel was scared and that we could help him with this confusing transition. He was more likely going to be moved from the foster home he was in due to his behaviors anyway. I thought it better if the next move was to our home.

Miguel struggled. For the first weekend he was home, my husband was away at his scheduled National Guard weekend. Miguel squeezed under a desk ten feet from me and cried and screamed and told me he was going to kill me and how he planned to kill me. I knew in my heart he was hurting. I decided to take a light hearted approach because that meshed with his natural personality. In the next few years, he would periodically have these episodes. Although I felt for him, I did not know what to do or who to turn to. We generally used humor, structure and normalcy to prevent and deal with these outbursts. He was a good boy. He was fun with a great sense of humor, but when something set him off he would act this way. In the car one day, he had a fit of rage and declared that he was going to jump out the window. Back in those days, we had a Caravan and anyone who remembers the Caravans, know the back windows did not open all the way. They opened sideways about two or three inches at best. As James and I looked back at this threat, James whimsically stated that "even Gumby could not fit through that window." Well, the entire car full erupted in laughter, and even Miguel in his fit of rage saw the humor in what he had said and finally gave in to laughter.

Our approach was a simple one, more logical than psychological. We normalized his life with no therapists or counselors. (Nothing against these professionals - this was simply the approach my husband and I took. We were also unfamiliar with how to find a therapist or counselor familiar with the needs of our adopted children.) We also believed in closure. We took him to visit previous foster homes, even one of his foster/adoptive homes, as we had with our first three boys.

We addressed his fits of rage with love and understanding of his fears and confusions, but eventually felt he deserved more consequences because he was not putting any effort into preventing these episodes. After one fit of rage, James and I decided to take snacks away. When Miguel was done, we all sat in the living room with his favorite dessert in our hands, chatting about good old times, good memories and fun things we have done together. Watching him out of the corner of my eye, he looked like a puppy being scolded. He was longing for a bite of that delicious looking dessert, but we knew we could not give in. He went a week without snacks. The lack of snacks bothered him immensely. He would ask throughout the week; how many days were left until he could have snacks. He made that week seem like a lifetime. Thankfully, that was the last of his fits until about a year later, when he went on a vacation with my parents and their young foster and adopted children. He had another fit of rage. I am guessing the insecurity of going with someone else, with someone else's expectations and someone else's routines, deregulated him. It most likely reminded him too much of his foster-care years and not knowing what family he was waking up to each morning.

We talked about his life before adoption and he would say, "You knew I did that and you still adopted me?" with complete amazement. We would say simply, "Yes." Each comment we made about his past, he would say the same thing and we would answer the same way. He never could grasp that we loved him anyway, and we loved him unconditionally. He needed the security of adoption and loved to hear his adoption story: when we first heard of him, why we chose him, what we thought, what we did, and any other details we could remember about the event. The night before his adoption day, he cried in our arms. He told us he was deathly afraid that the judge was going to disagree with the petition to adopt him. Even as we explained to him that it was finished and the adoption day in front of the judge was a mere formality, he did not understand it or believe it. He needed that piece of paper. He needed proof that the adoption was finalized and no one could prevent it.

Years later when his sister, who we adopted separately, ran away from our home because of her debilitating PTSD (Post traumatic Stress Disorder), Miguel completely lost it emotionally, spiritually, and psychologically. His security was broken. His safety was gone. I think he believed it had all been a lie. He now believed that his "forever" adoption was fragile and breakable. Miguel is 27 years old, and I still smile when I think of him. He was fun. He had a sense of adventure. He convinced me to do things I knew I should not do. One day, he convinced me to jump off of an icy snow bank for an alley-oop into the basketball hoop outside of our country home. He made it look simple. As I was in midair, I remembered our age difference and remembered how much harder I fall than he does. All I can say is, "It hurt," and I limped to the house in pain. He also taught me how to snowboard, but midway down the small country hill, my excitement made me fall forward. I wish there had been more snow to cushion the fall.

I am glad he kept me young. I am glad he enjoyed including me in his fun. I am saddened that with all that we did for him and with him, all the time we sat with him and talked to him, he never let go of stealing and deception. Because he was such a good-looking fun guy, he became a good con man. It took me years to realize the fullness of it. It took me years to realize that when he offered to buy me a Pepsi and absolutely insisted I accept his offer, it was because he had stolen the money from me in the first place and felt the need to spend some of it on me. Throughout his childhood, he stole any food or candy in a wrapper that he could and would save the wrapper in one of his shirt pockets hanging in his closet or backpack as if he was holding all of the wrappers as trophies. Amazingly, he would deny stealing even when confronted with a pile of wrappers. As an adult, he carried his drive to steal, and it ultimately landed him in jail a few times.

Over My Dead Body

When Jadin was eight years-old, Miguel ten, Drake twelve and Kyle seventeen, James and I took them camping at a campground near their home county for a week for the sole purpose of visiting with people these children felt attached to in different ways to different extents before being adopted by us. We believed in continuing close relationships, as well as closure for these hurting children. We wanted their losses in their life to be minimized. This is when we met Miguel's younger sister. We had invited her to go hiking with us, but the foster mother did not trust her to stay on the trail and not fall off the cliff-like ledge of the glen. I thought it odd as she was nine years old, but I could not convince the foster mother to let her go with us. She did bring her over one evening to the campground before bed. I would like to say it was a nice visit, but the little girl was an ungrateful and spoiled handful. When her foster mother said no to videogames, she forcefully turned her foster mother's head, squeezed her cheeks, and demanded money. I stared in disbelief. My husband was disgusted. The foster mother gave her the money. I felt pity for this little girl. It is a disservice to a child when they are that grossly undisciplined. It was obvious this young girl had more power than a little girl her age should ever have. It scares a child to have this much power. Children, especially foster and adopted children, need to feel secure in the loving arms of strong parents.

It was no secret that James and I were looking to adopt a girl. We felt that a girl would soften the hearts of the boys and make for a well-rounded family. A friend told me that I was not yet a parent because I had not had any girls. It hurt my feelings, but I understand her now. A girl changes the dynamics and adds estrogen and a roller coaster of emotions, as well as drama and nail polish to the mix of testosterone, basketball, sweat and obnoxious humor.

I spent countless hours on the internet looking for a girl to adopt. I found myself inquiring excitedly about several sibling groups with boys and girls. This avenue became as disappointing, time-sapping and heart-wrenching as the adoption blue books. In our frustration with this avenue, we alerted our previous case workers of our desire to adopt a girl, but in an epiphany, James announced that it would not be right to adopt a girl we did not know, when our son Miguel's little sister was adoptable. He felt that it would send the wrong message to Miguel and it would do more harm than good. We knew Miguel worried about his sister and wanted his sister to find an adoptive home like he had. He wanted his sister to find the same happiness and security he had, but he never mentioned us adopting her. We knew it bothered him and was overwhelming at times. I could not imagine her in our home. Her insensitivity, selfishness, deceitfully cruel demeanor, and spoiled rotten attitude made her a poor fit for our family (or any family). My response to James's announcement that we should adopt Jesslyn, was "Over my dead body," and I thought about how real that could become if we adopted her. She was not a pleasant girl in any respect. The special program she was in rewarded her with a $300 stereo for being good for a week and a pair of roller blades with a roller blade bag for another good week. I knew we could not keep up with that. The program she was in for difficult children also told her foster parents to leave the house if Jesslyn had a fit of rage. In one fit, Jesslyn proceeded to take all of the foster parents' pictures off the walls and smash them on the floor. When the foster parents entered the home prematurely, the foster mother got a telephone thrown at her face, breaking two teeth. Jesslyn was also known to kick the foster father's back. He spent the majority of his time in a wheel chair so he became Jesslyn's easy target for her unyielding anger. James believed that, with higher expectations, Jesslyn would rise to the occasion.

James convinced me. He won me over with the compassion I had for difficult children, and Jesslyn certainly was a difficult child. With a U-Haul of belongings and a fistful of daily medications, she sheepishly walked into our life and our home.

In the beginning, it was as if Miguel was her parent. She was stuck to him like glue. He became more and more agitated because he was an independent kind of a guy, used to doing as he pleased and melting in with the guys. He did not want a ten-year-old girl hanging on him. He complained to me in distress. I explained to him how she must feel. Even though they were not raised together in the same foster homes, did not resemble one another, and did not know each other, he was her only connection to her new adoptive family. I then dealt with her. I explained to her that Miguel needed some space and that we were her parents now. I began including her in cooking, baking, doing nails and playing dolls. She did fine. She accepted our rules, expectations and demands. This blue-eyed, blonde-haired girl won our hearts. She was surprisingly pleasant and compliant, and seemed to enjoy having a family.

School presented a challenge because she was accustomed to a 6:1:1 class, meaning there were six children, one teacher and a therapist. She explained that at least one child was restrained each day due to behavioral problems. Our goal was to normalize her life. She was homeschooled, like all of our other children, and her reading went from inconsistent first grade level to a solid fifth grade level in a short time. She enjoyed reading after she felt more confident. Her behavioral problems were almost non-existent, although there was an aroma of rebellion despite her compliance and goodness. Many times she seemed to remain on the outside looking in. She did not completely join the family. She remained somewhat unattached. Later, we learned how attachment disorder can destroy relationships and nearly an entire family.

So Soon

Before the finalization of our first daughter, Jesslyn, the county we had recently moved to, called us about two little girls ages eight and nine. We were told their names, that they were Puerto Rican, and that the older girl felt rejected. The older girl desperately wanted a family, so she would not be picked on or labeled as a foster child. She was sick of being called a foster child. I could relate to her need for a family – this is why I was driven to adopt rather than do foster care.

At that time, we were having a great deal of trouble with our older son, the first boy we adopted, Drake. He was now fourteen years old and was showing his true colors. We were struggling to show him the right way to go in life. We saw he was heading for prison, and we wanted desperately to convince him that our way lead to a better life.

We meant well but, looking back, I believe we were trying too hard. We needed to step back from his problem behaviors: fire-starting, sexual deviance, lying and stealing. We did not lose sight completely of the root of these behaviors, but we needed to love him where he was at. I think the distrust and anger shown through our eyes, more than the love of Jesus. We knew that he should not be out of our sight as it was not safe for us, the other children, or himself, but we lost track of trying to understand him and the root of these behaviors. We were busy looking at the behaviors, but who could blame us? His behaviors were often life-threatening. We were strictly in survival mode at the time with no life jackets. No one could help us. No one would help us. Criticize, judge, stare, yes, but help us? No one knew how.

In public, Drake looked like a model citizen, opening doors for old ladies, politely speaking to adults, taking the hand of young children and doing everything we asked him to do without complaint. At home, when no one was looking, he was a different person. We could not consider getting a babysitter due to his dangerous and immoral acting out.

33

On one occasion, we asked James's older sister to watch the boys. She was thrilled, but when we came to pick the boys up, she was exasperated and fearful. While in the bathroom, Drake had gotten into the cleaning supply closet and not wanting to get caught, threw all the cleaning supplies back in there quickly, along with a lit match. Thankfully, nothing happened. He was Dr. Jekyll and Mr. Hyde. It was scary because it only took a second for him to change, and there did not seem to be a trigger for this behavior.

Two years after Drake's adoption we moved into my dream house in the country. The house had seven gables, a wraparound porch, majestic doorways and beautiful woodwork. Our first night there, we were all exhausted from moving. We had worked extra hard to get all of our belongings moved into our new home and have everyone's beds set up in their respective rooms. We were tired and collapsed in our beds at about 10pm. At midnight, we heard boisterously-loud preaching downstairs. We could not make out exactly who it was or what the man was saying. James put me in front of him, thinking that a woman's softness and sweet talk could save our family. I disagreed, but went with him stuck to me like Velcro behind me. We reluctantly walked down the stairs, following the man bellowing something about Jesus. We rounded the corner and headed to Drake's room, confused. As we walked in and turned the light on, we saw that the alarm clock had gone off at midnight as it was not set to the proper time when it was plugged in and no one had made sure the alarm was off. Unfortunately, it was not that simple as it never was when Drake was involved. We smelled smoldering smoke.

Drake was sleeping hard. He had a history of doing this after he had done something wrong. It was as if his internal fears, sadness, anger and confusion were set free and relaxed by the act of fire starting. We fought to wake him up to ask him where the fire was. In his grogginess, he refused to tell us. It was his way, to initially lie and then, a year or so later, he would sit down and confess everything he had done wrong in the past. He had a glimmer in his eye as he would tell you the details, such as where you were when it happened. He seemed to enjoy explaining how he got away with it and how bad the action was with an exaggerated apologetic look on his face. It was nothing new when he refused to tell us about this smoldering match smell, but we did not have this kind of time. It was an emergency. We begged him, we slapped his arm, we threatened him, and we got in his face. We were scared. This was our home at stake and he had placed the family in grave danger. All of our other children were sleeping upstairs. Finally, thank God, James looked down into a hole in the rough wood floor and found a smoldering match in a layer of dusty flaked wood.

Drake's behaviors worsened and we held on tight. Our days were spent ensuring everyone's safety and the safety of our home in general. Our nights were spent praying we would wake up to see another day, even though there was a part of us that would rather not. It was clear he refused to obey society's rules, as well as any household rules. It is hard to admit, but there were times, when I thought of driving the car with him and I in it into a nearby tree at high speeds – thinking it was a way to protect my family. I feared that I would die, and he would live to continue to torment my husband. This fear kept me from following through with it. The desperation, fears and anger overpowered any love and understanding we had for him. The love was still there, but we could not access it because we were in survival mode. We were also trying to get him help. I tried to find a Scared Straight Program for fire starters, but no one knew anything about it. We did get him a psychiatrist, but he did not seem to be overly anxious to address Drake's needs. He was put on an anti-depressant which made him a happy criminal and seemed to enhance his sexual desire. We did not understand why a child would not want a family to call his own, even if it was not the family he chose.

Survival mode is a state of being that limits a person's potential to think, reason, or imagine. It is a time when our world becomes small, and we are unable to think beyond the immediate problem or moment. To do anything beyond this would take a great deal of concentration and effort. The survival mode often includes memory loss, agitation, fear and confusion. I have forgotten important information, appointments and routine. Survival mode is stressful and can be dangerous. It has caused me to do atypical, dumb things because it is nearly impossible to access any higher thinking or alertness during this time. Driving, which is a normal daily activity for most people, can become compromised with this lack of concentration and alertness. It is scary.

One cannot imagine what it was like to live with and to raise Drake unless they have had a child like him. We wanted so much for him, but he did not seem to want anything for himself. We wanted to love him, but he would not let us into his world. Or, perhaps we did not know how to reach him and we were angry because he would not reach out to us. When we got the call about two little hurting girls, my heart broke. I wanted them, but my logical, unyielding husband was hesitant to add young girls to our family with Drake's issues. I begged and pleaded. I explained that I could do it. After all, when we want something bad enough, we feel we can do anything, similar to a superwoman attitude. James gave in. He too, was taken by their description and the older girl's desire for a home. He too, was excited about adding to our family. My only hesitation now was the realization that the washer would now be working overtime.

The next day, I called the county back and told them we would adopt the two little girls.

"Oh no, we are looking for a foster family that is dually certified as an adoptive home, not necessarily a home that will adopt them."

I said, "Right. We are an adoptive home. We are not a foster home. You did not call a foster home. We would like to adopt them."

"But you have not met them yet."

"Good point," I thought. Then I asked, "Why? Did you meet your children first?" I knew this worker had not adopted one child, let alone any of her children. My comment was met with silence for what seemed like several minutes. Finally, the voice on the other end of the telephone line agreed with me that she had not met her children before having them. It gave her a new perspective. After dealing with foster-adoptive workers for more than two decades, I see that they do not agree with adoption. They feel the children need to resemble the adoptive parents, and they do not feel that adoptive parents can truly love a child that is not their own. As a result, workers typically misunderstand families who have a troubled adopted child.

The girls' foster mother gave the County five days to get the children out of her home because she was getting divorced and could not handle the girls. Within two days, we met the girls. We had them over for pizza and went for a walk with them out back. We discussed what it would be like living with us. Their foster mother and the County decided we would pick them up for good two days later.

We had no idea how many belongings they would have, especially after picking up Jesslyn with a U-Haul. We arranged for James' and my fathers to help with the transition. I remained home with the other children, and our dads and James went to pick them up. To this day, the image of the two girls comes to mind when we deal with their childish, selfish, and mean ways. James cannot shake the vision of the fear in their eyes, the uncertainty of what lay ahead, and the rejection they displayed. They were so young, but had had to deal with so much pain and rejection. We wanted to fill that void for them, but we found out years later that they had already filled that void their way. They filled it with their rejection and the brick walls they built around their hearts, as well as a blurry perception of the world around them. The older girl was parentified. She controlled the younger girl's thoughts and perceptions of the world. The younger girl had become her puppet and was subject to her sister's demands. The younger girl was never allowed to have independent thoughts or grow up emotionally, spiritually or psychologically. At 22 years old, she still has not broken free from her older sister.

Brittani and Chloe joined our family, with all of their pains, sorrows and the baggage we would begin to hear about in the years to come. As with our older boys and Jesslyn, we believed in closure to help them with their loyalty issues and their transition. We continued to visit their foster mother occasionally through the years and invited her over to our house. Neither girl seemed to genuinely respect her or miss living with her, complaining mostly of the two older brothers, the foster mother's smoking habit, being put to bed early and "living at the babysitters." We attempted to promote respect regardless of their issues with her. Later on, we were stabbed in the back by the foster mother when we could have used the same type of respect.

Brittani, the older girl had no respect for her previous foster mother, but we encouraged her to respect her even if she did not warrant it. Through the next few years, we learned that she had little respect for any adults or authority figures in her life. We guessed this was due to her past abuse and neglect; her inability to trust others; and her unwillingness to forgive her birth mother.

When she was a teenager, we were given a small book on forgiveness at church and I encouraged her to read it. She scowled when she read the title and absolutely refused to read it. I explained that forgiving her mother would not mean accepting her mother's actions, but forgiveness frees both of you to be able to change. Forgiveness gives you peace and freedom. Sadly, she would not even touch the book as if it carried with it the bubonic plague.

The Wilderness

James and I went through many years of great loss and disappointment of several different kinds. We could relate to the Israelites and the Promised Land. The Israelites spent forty years walking around in circles because their hearts were not prepared for what God had for them. Our wilderness began with losing Drake, at age fourteen, four years after his adoption. Although he did not die, it felt like a death. In many ways, it felt worse than a death. When a child dies, others acknowledge your pain, and mourn with you and for you. There is a funeral and a wake, where people console you, leave cards for you and bring food. A funeral helps you deal with your loss. When an adopted child leaves prematurely due to emotional difficulties and behavioral issues, outsiders are quick to judge, criticize and condemn, but do not acknowledge an adoptive parent's loss and need to mourn.

Our family was traumatized. We experienced numerous, mixed and confusing emotions. On one hand we had a sense of peace and relaxation that we had not had in the four years since Drake joined our family. We had to be FBI agents and we had to be aware of every move Drake made. He was an opportunist. If he had a couple seconds, he would take the opportunity to do something nasty, illegal, gross, or wrong. We had to be aware of where he and the other children were at all times because of his sexual aggression. It was taxing and prevented us from having a normal home life.

With the peace of him leaving, came bitterness and anger. We had given him our lives, finances, open hearts and excitement to be parents, and he in turn stepped on our hearts. He threw our sacrifices away as if it was all garbage. It was not garbage. We had a lot of love to give, and we had a desire to give it away. We wanted his adoption to end in a healthy transition to independence. We wanted to maintain an on-going relationship as he transitioned. Unfortunately, it was not to be.

Dreams of raising Drake to independence ended as abruptly as they began. One day, while keeping Drake on an "Adults Only" status for severe behavior issues, he made a decision. He decided he was finished with us and finished with abiding by our rules. While sitting with me, talking to me as I painted a door, a fraction of our 5000 square foot home, he began to confess. His confession made my jaw drop.

My son Drake had just admitted to having an ongoing sexual relationship with another boy whom we knew well. I was confused and disgusted. My head was swimming. I was alone that week as my husband was away at a two-week training for National Guard.

I was angry that we had unwittingly allowed him to be alone with the other boy long enough to do such things. Because of his background and his behaviors in our home, we were always careful. How could we have been so careless? We were regularly accused by other parents of being too hard on Drake and being too alert to what he was up to. We did not tell everyone about his history or behaviors. As a result, friends, family and others did not understand. Even those we did tell, did not understand - Drake was a model citizen in front of them.

We were continuously criticized by others. Despite our vigilance, he had not only repeatedly lied, stolen, manipulated, urinated out his window, and started fires in our home, but he has also sexually abused a good friend. We were humiliated.

The thought of telling the victim's unsuspecting parents made me sick to my stomach. I could not fathom where to start, but somehow, by the grace of God, I did. They took it well, and immediately sought counseling for their child. We also sought counseling for Jadin, Drake's younger biological brother. In the three years of counseling, Jadin had never made any measured strides towards advocating for himself, communicating effectively, or addressing his adoptive issues such as insecurity or abuses. We were disappointed with our attempt to help Jadin open up.

After Drake's unexpected confession of an ongoing sexual relationship with a boy, the following days are a blur. I do not remember the exact turn of events, but the trooper whom I called, stood in front of me, writing down my answers to his questions about Drake's sex offending. He asked me how I found out about this on-going sexual abuse. Without thinking, I replied, "He told me." For a moment, I had forgotten that this was not normal. The trooper abruptly stopped writing, looked up at me, and incredulously asked, "What?" He sounded so incredulous, it knocked me back to reality. I explained to him that Drake operates this way all the time. When he has done something wrong, he waits an undetermined amount of time, and then confesses to most of the facts, but never all of the facts as he does not want to give away his tactics and thought patterns.

Drake's confessions were a way for him to brag about what he had done. The trooper was still in awe, but continued a bit more slowly now. Soon, the sex abuse task force was on the case. They were surprisingly unprofessional and were obviously not accustomed to talking to people who had developmental delays like the victim. Despite every indication that Drake had carefully selected and groomed his victim, the sex abuse task force declared that Drake and the victim had had a mutual relationship. Drake was not held accountable. However, he was assigned to go to probation on admissions status as a way to try to scare him straight. In reality, it was another way to show our son that what he did was not that bad. I wanted him to experience accountability for his actions and choices and get the help he so desperately needed, but he was not even officially placed on probation. I could not find anyone sympathetic to my cause or who understood the severity of the situation.

During his second probation appointment, I spoke to the probation officer before my son was invited in. I asked the probation officer some pointed questions and wanted truthful answers. I asked, "If Drake can steal, manipulate, lie, start fires in our home on multiple occasions and sexually abuse a developmentally disabled boy and get away with it; when he kills me, will he at least be a suspect? I know that he cannot automatically be accused, but will he at the very least, be looked at as a possible suspect because that is next and I want to be sure he is a suspect. I am not worried about dying at the hands of an adoptee, but it does concern me that he would get away with it without even being considered."

I never looked away from the probation officer while I asked these questions, nor did I show any fear or emotion – I wanted him to have a sense of the state of affairs at home. I will never forget the look on his face. He stared in disbelief and awe that I could ask such questions without any fear or concern for my life. It was simply reality. His gaze did not leave my eyes, as he slowly picked up the telephone on the corner of his desk. He obviously had memorized where the telephone sat. He spoke in a few short sentences to the person on the other end and hung up, while he continued to stare.

After the call, he announced that Drake would have an emergency court hearing tomorrow for juvenile delinquents. To any normal family, that sounded fast and helpful. To me, it sounded like Drake had one more day to accomplish the task at hand. I have to admit I was a bit scared, but decided to give my fear to my God and get a good night's sleep that night.

In the prior months, I had seen where Drake was headed, and he was going downhill quickly. Since we adopted Brittani and Chloe, his behavior was getting worse. He was making sexual gestures through the windows if he was outside and the girls were inside. He would keep his eyes open during family prayers at night and look the girls up and down, as if inappropriately checking them out. The other children, especially the girls, were getting scared and having nightmares. I spent hours counseling them about their fears and trying to keep them safe from these fears becoming reality. Interestingly, Brittani and Chloe were not good candidates to be victims because of their outspoken personalities and strong morals. They were definitely a good fit for our family.

Drake groomed his victims like any good predator. While testing out the waters with each of our girls, he found that they immediately told on him and outwardly expressed disgust, causing attention to be drawn to him and his deviant behaviors. That is not what someone like him wants. He was not concerned about being caught or consequences, but he enjoyed the deceit, sneakiness and the elated feeling from committing his crimes. Even the probation officer attempted to scare him straight. A large uniformed police officer took Drake away with a sly look on his face and put him into a jail cell, dramatically slamming the door shut on Drake. Several minutes later, the large officer no longer looked so large. His face was no longer sly, but white with fear and concern as he stated that the scare tactic did not bother Drake in the least. I had already explained to them that Drake would react that way, but I guess when people see if for themselves it makes more of an impression.

Over the years, we have found that people cannot understand how bad our lives were because they had never lived with someone so cruel, destructive and evil-minded. Worse yet, people would equate their parenting experiences with the craziness and fear that we were living on a day to day basis. They would compare their biological child who occasionally lies, to my child. I would stare in disbelief of their ignorance and inability to hear what I was saying. I became envious of people that did not understand because I knew it meant they had never lived it. I also felt pity for my children because their trauma and past abuses were continually minimized and compared to normal behavior. The older generation refers to these hopeless children as having "bad blood." This reference appalled me, but now I understand that some things our children struggle with are genetic or generational, whereas other behaviors and struggles are nurtured or learned. While I secretly wish there was no truth to it, I no longer get angry when people use the bad blood reference.

After Drake left our home, our troubles with him did not end. While Drake was in a sex offender rehabilitation residence, we were charged with abuse for the first time. It was embarrassing and struck us to the core. It occurred soon after we told Drake over the telephone that given his sexual tendencies and past, he would never be welcome to live with us again. As with everything in his life, Drake was shocked and dismayed by such a significant consequence to his choices. I am sure it angered him and frightened him as he now had no plans of where to go after the sex offender rehab, but we had no choice. We had not been allowed to meaningfully participate in his treatment. We had little contact with Drake while he was in rehab. He was old enough, and exercised his

43

right, to discontinue any progress reports to us. We did not know if this treatment was alleviating his deep desires or sexually deviant thoughts and behaviors.

Professionals involved in his treatment kept us on the outside looking in, withheld information, and treated us like second-class citizens. Despite being in a treatment program for sex offenders, the treatment facility offered no additional information about the extent of his sex offending. They were intent on turning our child against us, rather than re-building our relationship with Drake and our family. The more we tried to be involved in his treatment and decisions, the more we were pushed away with insults, criticism and judgment. Any residential facility or court documents were speckled with untrue, hurtful comments. There was no acknowledgement or respect for who we were, what the child put us through, or how hard we had tried. We also had several other children in our home at that time, and we were scared and unwilling to put them at risk for Drake – a child that never seemed to want to be part of our family or abide by simple rules.

During the abuse investigation, child protective treated us like criminals and we were screamed at on the phone by county case workers. Child protective assumes you are guilty and looks for the slightest facts to confirm their suspicions. Child protective acted like it was no big deal to be charged with abuse. We felt otherwise, as it affects our reputations, careers and standing in the church. We were subjected to random unannounced checks and cruel-hearted, mean-spirited case workers who had never had foster or adoptive children, nor had they ever dealt with sexual abuse or other criminal behaviors in the home. My brain is reactive and emotions quickly stir which prevents me from communicating effectively and addressing their contradictions and ignorance regarding the situation. Any attempts at trying to answer calmly and appropriately with truth, was shot down like an enemy plane, by a magazine of loaded questions. My head would spin as I tried to answer each question.

The most they knew of Drake was a picture on our wall. The more we tried to prove our innocence and provide open access to our home, the more they assumed we were guilty. It was a scary time for us.

We had five other children in our home all of whom had come from the foster care system and multiple disruptions, which made them vulnerable to insecurity. Their insecurity was fueled by watching the case workers question and undermine us in front of them.

Interestingly, I had a previous disagreement approximately five years prior to this abuse allegation, with this same child protective worker, regarding a former foster child in my mother's home. This topic was brought up in an unfavorable manner during her visit. Before that, she sat next to me in our graduation from college. When I asked for a new case worker due to the conflict of interest, they refused.

Amidst the abuse investigation, Brittani and Chloe participated in their adoptive placement meeting. During the meeting, their case worker pointedly exclaimed that our recent troubles with Drake could jeopardize "the placements." She reminded me that Brittani and Chloe were "the county's children" as if to threaten me that they could take my children away at any time. I stared back deep into her eyes and said:

"They are not placements. They are my children and you will not threaten me. You would destroy these children if you removed them from our home. I do not think that is what you want."

At another point, the child protective case worker stood screaming on our porch because I chose to exercise my rights and refused to let her into my home. In a planned meeting with the same case worker, she denied ever doing such a thing. Chloe glared angrily at this case worker and confronted her. She told the worker that it had scared her when she (the worker) screamed on our porch, but the case worker acted as if my daughter was making it up. Interestingly, during their 'full investigation' of the abuse allegation, child protective services never tried to contact our oldest son whom had recently moved out. Being 19 years-old, it seems he would have been knowledgeable about our home life.

I slipped into anorexia for a few months. I never imagined this would happen to me, but depression got the best of me. I was an emotional mess. My dreams were being shattered by one troubled child with extreme neglect, abuse and heartache in his background. We had been unable to reach him and the county had no clue about the severity of

45

his behaviors. We were not perfect parents, but we did not deserve to be harassed by the county. We were adoptive parents who were trying to reach a hurting child that everyone had given up on.

I wanted Drake to get the help he needed. I wanted him labeled so that he could not hurt anyone else and so that he could be given the proper treatment at the sex offender rehab. I wrote letters upon letters to the state and to the county, explaining what it was like raising this damaged child and how hard we had tried to fulfill his needs. I outlined his behaviors and the frequency of each behavior which extended far beyond his sexual abuse issues.

The Director of the Department of Social Services accused me of trying to get the case workers against my son when I listed his behaviors by severity. This sounded high-schoolish and never entered my mind. I thought I was talking to professionals, not teenagers easily swayed by gossip and emotion. Because I tried to advocate for Drake and insist that he be held accountable for his actions, I was considered unstable. Through my heartache and disappointment, I continued to write letters and make phone calls to state officials, the commissioner of our county, Drake's previous probation officer, and the attorney denying the sexual abuse case to follow through, our homeschool legal defense and the letter to the editor section of the newspaper. Many of these letters addressed to various people, were forwarded to child protective. Child protective then sent me threatening letters in return. I also began perusing the internet to help protect my family from CPS (Child Protective Services) and learn my parental rights as well as how to protect them.

I went down a never-ending painful road that led to a deeper depression. James handled his hurt differently. He concentrated more on what he could change than what he could not change. His heart was not in advocating or fighting. He saw it as a dead-end road and the people involved as a waste of his energies. Nevertheless, he occasionally sat down with me and helped me edit letters I wrote. In the end, we were found guilty of child abuse, but we appealed the county's findings to the State. We appealed based on their lack of evidence and their faulty paperwork. Inconsistencies and incorrect information was scattered throughout the accusation. The case worker documented our children as "Caucasian" rather than the mix of races they were. The case worker said that I "scared the children" before I allowed the case workers to speak with them, which caused my children to be "too scared to talk." When the county car drove into the driveway, Jesslyn saw it first. Her heart raced as she told me frantically who had driven in. She, of all of my children, was accustomed to the car with the state emblem stamped on its driver's side door. When they introduced themselves, I turned to introduce them to my children, and said that they wanted to speak with them. I then left them alone and immediately ran to a different room to call James. They never arranged for another meeting with my children to talk to them when they were calm. The case worker stated in the report that my children were "close by while we talked." I had sent them to their rooms which was in the other part of our 5000 square foot home, upstairs. I did not know I had to send them to Timbuktu, and at the time of our meeting they never mentioned any problem with where our children were located. They had little contact with James or me after this initial visit. Ironically, too, the paperwork accused us of "refusing services" despite the fact that services were never offered. Post-adoptive services did not even exist in our county. I had been begging for services, calling all over the state looking for any services any agencies had to offer.

Drake had falsified two police reports while attending public school when he was being investigated by a trooper for stealing Ritalin from the school nurse. Drake has demonstrated a willingness to resort to drastic measures when acting out his anger, such as starting fires and sexually abusing those we love. Drake lied to treatment providers in his sex offender rehab regarding his family history. For example, he claimed his biological father died of a drug overdose. There were numerous instances when Drake would lie out of anger and confusion.

We won our battle with the county. We submitted a single ten-page packet to the state as our appeal. We focused on identifying the county's numerous inconsistencies. We were relieved, but we were still in the midst of transitioning from being corrections officers to becoming parents for our five other needy children.

Their Growing Up Years

The growing-up years were uncomplicated. The children adjusted to our family and enjoyed their childhood- ages eight to fourteen were so simple. Kyle had gone to independence, Drake had gone to a group home after sex offender rehab, and James and I had Miguel, Jadin, Brittani, Jesslyn and Chloe at home. We played sports and board games together as a family. We played soccer where I was always a liability because I was not good. Softball was a different story; I proved to be more skilled. Our children always played on a soccer team so they were well-versed in fancy footwork, making goals, and passing the ball. Some of them were on a basketball team, and all of them took karate lessons. James coached several years of basketball and I took on the challenging job of operating the concession stand, providing much needed refreshments and home-made foods.

James and I greatly enjoyed being involved. We thought it was important for us to be at every game, and although we cheered too much at times, the children were grateful for our involvement and enthusiasm. Our main focus was to find something that suited each child's talents, natural abilities and dreams.

We frequently traveled together. We traveled four hours to visit James's aunt and enjoyed nearby historic sites, as well as local restaurants and river views. We traveled to distant states and attended NCAA basketball tournament games. We also visited relatives and enjoyed nearby sights. Our most organized trip, was to St. Louis, Missouri, the Gateway to the West. We went to the top of the Arch. We brought my parents and their adopted children with us because my mom always wanted to go there, but was not much of a traveler. From St. Louis, we went on to Branson, Missouri and rented a condominium. We saw several live shows including a western show, Dolly Parton's live horse show, and an oldies show. We also took a train ride and spent a day at an amusement park.

We also took several trips during the growing-up years to the seashore to visit relatives and enjoy the ocean. This destination was always a relaxing vacation because we parked the car for a week and enjoyed walking everywhere we went, along with the refreshing ocean breezes. Our kids relished in the freedom that came with it.

We loved to experience things together as a family. We willingly spent our money on building memories and reluctantly spent money on unneeded material items like new toys or new clothes. Like most American families, we had plenty. Several families consistently gave us beautiful brand name clothes that fit our children perfectly. This always angered Brittani. Although I explained to her that I would rather spend time with her than buy her unneeded new clothes, nothing I said mattered to her. We did, however, believe in brand name new sneakers and footwear. Once a year, we traveled to an outlet center to buy sneakers, cleats, sandals and socks. It is no fun to get new sneakers when you have old socks. Since it was an outlet center, there were numerous choices and we found what we wanted. In the end, or middle, depending on how much luck we had shopping, we ate at the food court. We usually bought something at the kitchen outlet store and sometimes the jewelry outlet store, depending on what caught our eye. It was a costly trip, but it was fun and we felt it was important for our children to grow up with traditions such as this.

I know we were too busy at times. Occasionally, Jadin would announce: "It is good to be bored sometimes." There were times that I felt guilty about our busy lifestyle, but overall we tried to have a balance. We tried not to be too busy. We tried to enjoy our outings and our time at home. We enjoyed sitting in the living room and chatting. The kids looked forward to movie nights where they organized the living room like a theatre as best they could, with blankets and tables for the popcorn and such. I would make several bowls of popcorn with either cheese sprinkled on it or salt and butter. Our biggest challenge was keeping the dogs out of the popcorn while we settled in to our seats for the movie.

Our children needed experiences to make up for what they lost as abused, abandoned and neglected children. We were engaged in our community as well as neighboring communities. We frequently went to art shows and followed up by writing letters to the artists. We read books and followed up by writing letters to the authors. We heard former United States President Jimmy Carter and Dr. Martin Luther King, Jr.'s daughter, Bernice A. King, speak at local colleges. We were able to meet with Bernice after her presentation. We went to professional and amateur plays and concerts and shows like the Harlem Globe Trotters, Jesus Christ Superstar, the local Symphony, and Rebecca St. James. We usually waited around after events so we would get a chance to meet people. I loved that our children were able to learn that these people on stage were regular people and that they too could aspire to whatever they felt led to, without their adoptive status holding them back.

For about five years, it seemed that everything we did was fun because we were together and we all got along well. Generally, the kids did not fight. We enjoyed each other's company, each other's differences and each other's individuality. As a mom, I loved to stop my busy Type A personality and sit on the front porch and watch them play. One of my favorite activities was when they all dressed up as cowboys and cowgirls and rode the jungle gym like it was a wagon from the pioneer days. That was Miguel's idea. He was extremely creative and always loved to dress up and pretend. Miguel and Jadin never fought. We often wondered if they were cousins by blood or family somehow as they got along famously. The girls would get jealous and bicker and fight, but overall, they all played together, not having time for arguing. I would smile and be thankful for being blessed – we were coming together and growing as a family.

James and I were happy. It was not all perfect, but we could handle the bumps and bruises along the way. We also tried to get to the root of some of the wrong thinking and wrong behaviors while they were young, including sexual behaviors, perfectionism, stealing and refusing to answer questions. We encouraged them to come to us if they had a problem or needed something. However, they had been independent at such young ages in their birth families and did not trust adults to fulfill their needs. They all had a tendency to take matters into their own hands because they had an underlying drive to fulfill their basic needs regardless of consequences. They frequently stole food and other items they wanted and lied. Jadin once missed an entire season of soccer because I asked him to communicate. I set the registration card on the table for all to see and told him all he needed to do, was let me know if he would like to do soccer that year. He never brought it up, regardless of my continuous reminders and explanations of my expectations. His stubbornness prevailed and his soccer skills suffered.

We tried hard to help them understand the role of parents and the role of children, by our actions as well as our words. We also wanted them to understand the role that a Heavenly Father plays in their life, but it was a difficult concept for children that felt like 'throw-aways' most of their life to grasp that an unseen Heavenly Father loved them dearly. God was too much like Santa Claus to them. We tried to show them His love by the way we lived and trusted in Him in hard times and our testimonies of times in our lives when we heard Him or felt His presence.

We understood that they had lived a life before coming to us. Unlike most adoptive parents we had met, we valued their birth families and their former lives and allowed them to express their concerns, process memories and fears. We listened to their stories even when we questioned the accuracy of their facts. We kept the adoption experience open through loving communication and consistently acknowledged the existence of their birth families. We traveled hundreds, sometimes thousands of miles, to reconnect and connect them with blood relatives and others they cared about. We understood that while they had gained much through adoption, they had also lost everything they knew before at the same time. We do not subscribe to the belief that children are a blank slate and can start a new life with no issues from their past. Adoptive parents cannot erase past hurts like a whiteboard. Their past is always a part of them and must be acknowledged and tended to gently, even if they were adopted at a young age.

We envisioned their adult lives and laughed out loud. We picked on Jadin because we all said he would serve us peanut butter and jelly, his all-time favorite food, if we went to his house to eat a holiday meal. We picked on Miguel because he would have a messy house as his room was always messy. We would joke that Jesslyn would have ten children because she liked children and we often found her reading baby name books. Interestingly, few of our children had reality-based life goals - they could not see themselves in the future. For example, Miguel insisted he would be an NBA basketball player someday. But while he was a good high school player, he did not have any extraordinary physical talent. Unfortunately, Brittani always stated she would live far away from us, in a secret place and in a secret house, never to be found again (not even by private investigators or her sisters). We laughed it off and told her we would find her, but we always felt a stinging pain in our hearts. We wondered why she would say things like that when we tried to show her unconditional love. We did sports, traveled, learned together and laughed together. Why at such a young age did she feel that way? We prayed it was just talk, but unfortunately, it was buried deep in her heart and she would never let that go. I think now, that it comes from her deep loyalty to a mother who only continually hurt her. Brittani could not let her birth mother go and therefore, could not allow herself to love someone again. She was waiting for us to hurt her as much as her birth mother had. She has never been able to forgive her birth mother, which has erected a permanent barrier between us.

A Year of Many Losses

Soon after the traumatic loss of Drake, we had a devastating year of losses. We had so many loved ones die that year that I think our children began to consider the funeral home a second home. Going to the funeral home became a normal outing or field trip. Also, the presence of evil in our household for nearly four years, had long-lasting effects that still impacted our daily lives.

I felt badly for my children, all preteens and teens at this point, but I could not shield them from life. Life is all about births and deaths. It was what was in between that mattered - life itself. James and I put in extra effort to help our children understand death, loss and grief. We quickly learned a loss of any proportion brought up the previous losses in their pre-adoptive lives. We stayed in close touch with them as they walked through this difficult part of life.

That year my little nine year-old brother was killed in a tragic accident. He had been close to our children, and they were crushed. James and I were devastated that we had lost someone so close and so young. We will never forget seeing him as he lay in the emergency room with rescue workers performing CPR until a doctor could pronounce him dead. We will never forget sitting our children down on our living room couch to tell them that their favorite playmate, Kelven, was dead. None of us had ever had a chance to say goodbye.

He was a child everyone loved, but sometimes could not stand. I absolutely adored this child all the time. I loved his personality, his sense of humor, his candidness, his honesty, and his smile. He was fun. One time, while at my house, all the children decided to go sledding across the street to the farmer's land where the hill was much larger and seemed to continue forever. I had stayed inside to bake fresh cookies and homemade hot chocolate, when Kelven arrived through the door, eyes open wide, panting. I had been surprised to see him so soon. As I examined his look of excitement and exhaustion, I noticed he had wet through his snow pants. Before I could say anything, he cut me off and declared, "I know what you are going to say. I did not wait too long to go to the bathroom." Then he hesitated and emphasized, "That hill is BIG." Apparently, the hill was too much for he and his bladder to handle.

He was honest to a fault. For example, when I asked him if he hit his brother with a golf club, he immediately admitted to it, with wide open eyes looking into ours. Many times, when dealing with him, I would have to quickly dive into corners or nearby rooms to chuckle or smile, and return to scold him firmly. He understood people's differences at a young age. When one of the children made a comment about Kelven enjoying visiting my house more than my sister's house, he got serious for a moment and stated emphatically, "Everyone's different. There are things I like at each house and I do not compare them. I love both of my sisters!" When I overheard him say that, I melted. Although, there is always a selfish, human part of you who wants to be more fun or better than the other guy, I was impressed with his perception and understanding of people and his love for everyone.

When I got the phone call he had been hit by a car, I felt numb. Fear enveloped me, but I went through the motions to ensure our children were taken care of and were safe to be left behind. James and I quickly drove to my parents' house where the accident had occurred. Kelven had been riding a bike with my father when he was hit by a car going southbound then hit by another car going northbound after being thrown from the initial impact. The accident happened right outside my parents' home. My Dad was unfortunate enough to be right behind him, watching it all happen in slow motion and yet so fast there was nothing he could do to stop the chain of events. This continues to haunt him in his sleep even 12 years later. Ironically, my parents' had recently moved a mile down the road to a smaller home, to escape the dangers of the road. I grew up only a few feet from the main road. My mother wanted to keep the boys off the main road and give them more room to play that would be far from the road. I think this caused a lot of bitterness and depression for my parents.

On the way to my parents' house I did not know if he was alive or dead, but a peace came over me. I was hoping that it was a peace saying that he was going to be fine. As James and I approached the house, my grandmother told me Kelven was not responding when he was taken away in the ambulance. I moved in shock. I did not feel and I could not feel. I robotically climbed back into the car with James to head to the hospital. God put a song on my heart that I sang while traveling to find my little brother. It was a children's song and not a particularly favorite one, but a meaningful one nonetheless, "He's my Rock, my Sword, and my Shield. He's the wheel in the middle of the field. He's the lily in the valley, the night and shining star. Makes no difference where you are, gonna get on my knees and pray, gonna pray until the day that Jesus comes." It is an upbeat song and it seemed odd to me that God gave me that song to meditate on during this time of fear and sadness. It gave me peace and I love the peace that comes from God because it cannot be explained or forced, it just is.

At the hospital, we found out that he was not breathing and my mother was in the room with his lifeless body. My body wanted to collapse in a heap. Sadness overwhelmed my entire being, but yet, the peace was still above me like a rainbow. I walked in to see my mom holding my brother's hand. I stood there awkwardly, not being able to move or say anything. I had never seen someone who had just died before, who had not been properly prepared for a showing by a funeral home. I did not know how to handle the emotions inside me or the numbness. I wanted to cry to show my mother how much I was hurting too, but the tears would not come. I could not cry when my father's mother died either when I was seven years old. I was so embarrassed that I was happy she was with the Lord that I hid in the bathroom and pretended to cry so I would look normal. This time might have been similar, but I think it was more of shock that held my tears back. I stood awkwardly looking at my brother whom I loved dearly. I wanted him to jump up and give me a hug. I wanted to pray over him and have his body come back to life. I wanted to sing, Jesus Loves Me to him because that was his favorite song, but my voice could not speak or sing. I was lost. I was taking classes to become a Christian minister someday, but I could not speak, feel or act.

My mother was the first to speak and she demanded quietly that I hold his hand. I did not want to hold his hand. I had never held the hand of a dead person. I never felt the need to, but I trusted my mother knew what was best. I gathered that that was one of her biggest regrets when she had previously lost my baby brother. She had never held him again after my father had rushed him to the hospital when he was found not breathing in his crib. I awkwardly walked over to Kelven's side and took his hand. I wish I could have done more. I wish I could have kissed him, but I knew he was gone. He had already left for Glory. A tinge of jealousy went through my body. Meeting the Lord as a believer will be beautiful. Kelven had a beautiful childlike faith. I was happy to be his Sunday school teacher who had helped him understand who Jesus was and to fall in love with Him.

I am grateful for the way our faith has given us the peace that surpasses all understanding. I would find myself crying at the drop of a hat. Seemingly nothing would provoke a cry or depression. I wanted to feel God's peace, but I was devastated, depressed and angry at God for taking Kelven away. I was working on my seminary degree and felt that God should have rewarded me for it. I felt that God should have warned me so that I could have spent more time with Kelven or hugged him more. I felt that I should have been warned because I was so close to God at that point in my life or at least I was trying to be. Obviously, it does not work that way, but I was angry at God nonetheless. While painting my downstairs bathroom one day, tears rolled faster than my paint brush. I could no longer see the wall or the shelving unit as God's Word began to permeate my mind and soul. I felt the Lord ministering to me with His Word and realized that it was a sermon, not just a song or scripture. I grabbed a pen and paper on a clip board, sat on the closed toilet seat in the bathroom, and began to write as fast as the Words were coming. Over the next few weeks, I delivered this sermon to several local churches and got awesome testimonies of how God used my sermon to heal years of pain in various individuals tucked in the congregations. I thank God for His healing Word.

A Miracle Amid Our Pain

I believe every child was and is a miracle, but this situation seemed to be an outright reminder that God answers prayers and cares about His children's needs. The miracle's name is Tonita, otherwise known as Toni. There was not a dry eye in the place when Toni was reunited with her older sisters, Brittani and Chloe. And God's timing was perfect. We all needed a miracle and our God knew that.

Brittani and Chloe knew they had a baby sister. They remembered taking care of her when they were only 4 and 5 and Toni was a baby. Chloe remembered dropping her sister on her head. After being adopted, it haunted Brittani and Chloe even more that they had a happy safe environment, while they had no idea where Toni was. They did not know if she was alive or dead. They did not know if she was with their birth parents, which would not have been a good situation. Their birth parents had been alcohol and drug-addicted since very young ages. Coming from Puerto Rico as children, they had lived in the heart of the city. Their mother turned to prostitution for money and their father was a violent drug dealer, eventually dying of AIDS after several long-term prison stays. Toni had a different father who also spent much of his adult life in prison and was drug-addicted. He also died of AIDS, and she was never able to see him again after adoption. Their mother had eight children, but Toni was her father's only child.

Many nights were spent consoling Brittani and Chloe. Questions and concerns about Toni's whereabouts continued to fill their young, troubled heads long into the night. They were scared for her. They had spotted memories of being home with their birth parents in the city, in the middle of the drug culture. Danger and hunger were a part of every-day life. They were used to not being nurtured or cared for properly. They remembered being independent when they were extremely young – at a time when they should have been dependent on their parents. At a time when they should have felt safe and secure in a loving family, they were hiding in a bedroom being told to be silent while the din of their mother being beaten by their father came from the other side of the door. When they should have been excited to get Christmas and birthday gifts, they were apprehensive about gifts because they knew they would be sold within days for drug money. We often prayed for their little sister and her safety. We also prayed that the Lord would lead her to us in the hopes that Brittani and Chloe could re-establish a relationship.

That prayer was answered one night a couple years after Brittani and Chloe's adoption. The week following Kelven's death we went to an old-fashioned tent revival in the middle of a cornfield in a nearby town. There was a guest speaker from the Netherlands who I am sure was fantastic. Now and then we would hear something he was saying, but much of the time was spent pointing out the people seven rows ahead of us. Brittani stared, whispering to James that she and Chloe had visited this woman's home with their mother and Toni's father. She remembered writing on her basement wall with crayon. Being a child's distant memory, it was a cute story, but when James noticed the little girl sitting with the family, he declared emphatically, but quietly, "Yeah, well, that little girl looks like Brittani." One of the girls in that family had turned to see us and seemed to have told the mother. Soon after, this family hurriedly got up to leave in the middle of the service.

James and the two girls immediately got up and chased them down outside the tent. He began speaking to the woman by explaining that the girls, Brittani and Chloe, seem to remember her. The woman hesitated nervously and replied, "Yes, I am Dedra," and as she spoke she turned the little girl to the front of her and announced, "And this is their little sister Toni." Onlookers outside the tent revival activity caught on to what was going on, realizing it was a miraculous reunion of blood sisters torn apart by life's circumstances, and began to smile and tear up. Our families exchanged telephone numbers, and Dedra agreed to let us visit with Toni soon.

A couple of days later, we picked up Toni for dinner at a local restaurant. We took several pictures and marveled about how beautiful she was, inside and out, as well as how much she looked like Brittani. At this point, Toni was five years old and Brittani and Chloe were ten and eleven. We enjoyed the visit and were sad when it was over, but Dedra promised that we could see her again that weekend. Several consecutive weekends turned into most every weekend. We picked her up and dropped her off. After picking her up, we would secretly throw everything she brought, including the bag she brought the clothes in, into the washer to be washed and dried before they were noticed to be missing. She and her clothes smelled like unwashed filth, and we keep a clean house. We have a chore chart to be sure the house is cleaned daily. James never wanted to be embarrassed to have friends or family over. Each visit, we made bath time fun with bubbles and toys and washed her body and hair. Our weekends were fun, full of activity and enjoying each other.

Four months after meeting Toni and developing a relationship with Dedra, Dedra gave us contact information for the girls' big brother, Vinito. We excitedly contacted him and quickly arranged a visit with him five hours south of us. He gave us their birth parents' information, so that we could reunite the children with them. Their big brother reminded both James and I of our youth, and our dreams, a piece of us that seemed to have been lost in our adoptive parenting experiences and heartache. We felt old in some ways, but we had not lost our flexibility and sense of adventure. We would travel the ten-hour roundtrip many times, even as a day trip, to establish a relationship with their big brother. We enjoyed introducing this city boy to country pleasures like picking out pumpkins in the fall, snowmobiling and sledding in the winter, and taking walks in the forest in the summer. It was exciting to see his face light up at each new adventure or experience.

Wilderness Again

As much as it was exciting to have met Vinito, our lives were stagnant and seemed to come to a halt after our year of losses. The wilderness in our life was a time of wandering with no purpose or understanding of what was going on, much like the Israelites in the Bible. They wandered. Now and then they listened to their leader, Moses. Other times, they ridiculed Moses and wanted more than what God was providing for them. (Exodus)

I became depressed because I wanted to adopt more children. At this point in my life, when the children were teenagers, I wanted a baby. I had always wanted to adopt one baby. Before this, I felt that our life was too chaotic and I was too active for a baby to nap and have the peaceful home life he would need to grow healthy and well adjusted. I felt that now our family would be an ideal adoptive family for a baby to grow up in.

Gathered together on our bed with the children, watching the lightning strike across the sky over the hills in the distance, we all chattered about the possibility of a newborn baby in the family. I relished everyone's excited chatter, making our intimacy at that moment more meaningful. I enjoyed these moments with my children. Meal times, family meetings and informal gatherings such as these, brought us together as a family and created the unity that we all longed for.

In our search for a baby, James and I applied to private agencies. I spent hours organizing one page of pictures of our family followed by a letter to a potential birth mother. This one page would represent our family, what we had to offer a child, and why we should be chosen over the hundreds of people desiring a newborn. We were told by agency social workers that most adoptive parents refused to consider a baby if the mother admitted to drug or alcohol abuse. We were also told that most adoptive parents would not consider twins. We were ready for almost any challenge which set us apart. Birth parents would choose us several times in the next three years as a possible match, but turn us down in the final decision. Twice we were close to being chosen for twins, only to receive that dreaded phone call that we were not chosen after all.

The greatest heartbreak was when we were matched with a birthmother and had only an hour to prepare for the traveling. We rushed to the bank for a cashier's check and advance on a credit card only minutes before the bank was closing for the weekend. We then traveled four hours and left the children with an aunt. We bought a car seat on the way. We drove another six hours, arriving in the city. The baby girl was born in a neighboring state. On the way to visit the baby, we made plans for me to stay in a hotel for several weeks until the baby was cleared to cross the state border.

Walking into the hospital room with our agency social worker, we were greeted awkwardly by the mother of the baby and her mother. The twelve-year-old girl between them was the newborn baby's older sister. The older sister had been raised by her grandmother because the mother was into partying rather than parenting. We held the baby that was soon to be ours. We talked a bit to the birthmother, but there seemed to be a connection missing. The facilitator of the meeting was not good at bringing us together. In an attempt to help the birthmother feel comfortable, the social worker from the private agency, asked her what she had named her baby girl. I was confused. It left me bewildered and unable to formulate my thoughts. I always thought it was the adoptive parents who chose the name. I did not know that the birthmother is encouraged to choose a name and then the adoptive parents rename the child on adoption day. This seemed pointless if the birth mother is sure of the adoption process as her choice of action. James and I had trouble making conversation, asking questions or making a connection. Whatever connection was missing with the birth family; it was there with the baby girl in my arms. She was a beautiful six-pound baby, healthy and gorgeous. I do not think all babies are beautiful, but she was. As I looked into her beautiful eyes, I was anxious to start our life together, but I felt something was wrong.

The next morning, at the hotel, we were notified by a quick phone call, that the birthmother was having doubts about putting up such a beautiful baby for adoption. Her friends were telling her not to put the baby up for adoption. Although we were crushed, James and I had both felt it in our time together the evening before. The greatest heartache was knowing that the baby was going straight into foster care if the birthmother did not choose adoption. We were not aware of the details, but we knew she had not raised her other two children. Her mother had. She was into the party life and had tested positive for HIV. She was young and influenced by emotion rather than what might be best for her baby girl.

The next morning at the hotel, the morning we were to pick up our new baby girl, we got a call that the birthmother did not want us to adopt her baby. I cannot express my sadness and frustration. I was frustrated at the agency that they could not negotiate with her better with perhaps more of an open adoption option. I was frustrated that we could not talk to the birthmother one more time to see if there was some way we could reassure her that we would be a good home and good parents for the baby. But it was what it was, and I had to believe God's hand was in it, even if it felt like needles in my heart. James admitted that the most difficult thing for him was when he had to take the car seat back to the store for a refund. He said he nearly cried in the store. Driving to James' aunt's house without the baby was awkward. Telling the other children was difficult. We knew this disappointment would be another brick in their wall of disappointments. When adoptive parents choose to adopt, it deeply affects the family. When an adoption is disrupted it, too, deeply affects the family. That is why we did not share every up and down of adoption with the children. It would have been too hard on their already weakened hearts, but this one had looked like a reality.

The agency did not follow up with us regarding our loss. I felt they should have called us, written us, or expressed compassion for us. We had made all the necessary arrangements, traveled, and held our new baby, only to say goodbye to it all, yet there was silence from the agency.

At one point in our adoption journey, I called the designated case worker about adopting a beautiful five-year-old boy on her case load. The case worker was pleasant and she ended the conversation with a statement that changed everything. She said, "I will put your application with the others." I hesitated, then slowly asked her what she meant by her statement. She explained that she collects applications for several months from different parents that want to adopt the child, and then she gathers them, reads them all and makes a decision which prospective adoptive parent will be the new parent of the child. I immediately was appalled and told her to take my application out. I explained to her that I only wanted the children no one else wanted. She was silent.

At this point, with many losses, I began to become depressed and judgmental. I would often look at a pregnant woman with disdain. I would see children running the streets at a young age and feel the unfairness in my heart. I wanted desperately to adopt a baby, and many people have children and do not take care of them properly. I was disgusted with people that had several young children, only to see them pregnant again. I began to think about having a birth child, which I had never done in my life. It was not what I wanted to do in my life. My purpose in life was to care for the unwanted children. I did not want to add to the population, but I wanted one baby experience. I began wondering what God had in store for us. If I was at a restaurant with James and the kids, I imagined a young lady approaching us, seeing how happy we all were, and asking us if we would raise her child as our own. I imagined this scenario often.

In the next few years, craziness hit our home, and I began to realize why God might not have us adopt a baby right then. But James and I were getting older and we wanted a baby while we had the energy to play. We were torn with God's intentions for our family and His decisions. Did this mean, that we would never be given a newborn baby to raise? This reality scared me.

63

Steps Taken

Four years after having Toni for nearly every weekend, Dedra began using Toni's visit with her biological sisters as punishment. If we seemingly did something wrong, we were punished with no visit that weekend. If Toni displayed bad behavior in school or at home, visits with her sisters were taken away for the weekend. When four months went by with no visit, we began to worry about Toni and her welfare in the home she was in. Toni was not doing well with Dedra anymore. James and I had never believed in taking someone's child or fighting for them until now. Children feel torn and stuck in the middle and are forced to make decisions they are not mature enough to make. I did not believe in adopting a child someone else wanted.

We felt the need and desire to gain custody of Toni. Many reasons prompted this decision: inconsistent visitations, Toni's filth and unkempt hygiene, her sad and despondent attitude when being dropped off, her joy to be with our family, her biological sisters' need to know Toni is in a place that loves her and takes care of her basic needs, and that she did not have a bed to sleep in at Dedra's house. Dedra also had stated that Toni was having fits in school and alerting officials and CPS (child protective services) to check out her home. Toni said that the shower had tiny flying bugs in it and that she would pretend to take a shower when told to, but was too grossed out to take a shower. She also said that they all shoved everything under beds and in closets when the child protective workers would check out their home, because they do not check those places. We were scared that if the foster care system gained custody of Toni we would lose her forever. Additionally, it was of grave concern to both James and I that Toni was not in legal custody to anyone and had no medical insurance, dental insurance, or medical care. She also bragged about not having a proper seat in Dedra's car and of lying across her siblings, laying on the floor or even being stuffed in the trunk. When we approached the subject of adopting her and allowing Dedra to have visitations, Dedra would say that she "discussed the matter in depth with her Christian counselor and they both felt like the answer was 'no.'"

We continued visits with Toni when Dedra allowed them. Eventually, we contacted a lawyer who drew up legal custody papers for Toni.

Through the girls' big brother, whom we adored and treated like a son, we met Toni's birth parents. Brittani and Chloe were said to have a different father, who died a few years back, while in prison. Brittani and Chloe always used this as a reason not to treat Toni like a biological sister. She was only a half-sister in their eyes. James met with Toni's parents in the city. He took pictures, visited, and discussed the option of having us adopt Toni. Her father was reluctant to have Toni take on our last name, but when James suggested she keep his last name for her middle name, he agreed. He despised the idea of Toni living with Dedra, as did Toni's mother, but they did not have the resources to go get Toni and bring her back with them, nor did they have the courage or the proper home life. Dedra intimidated them.

James's visit with them went well and we set up a visit with the girls to see their mother and step-father. This was to be a significant step in Brittani and Chloe's life. The last time they saw their mother, she had said she would be right back and never came back. Brittani and Chloe were only about four and five years old when they last saw their mother, ended up with several different relatives and then were dumped into the foster care system. Brittani and Chloe, their birthmother, their stepfather and their biological brother were filled with an array of emotions and unforgiveness, but James and I felt that a meeting would help them have closure in that part of their lives. Dedra insisted that Toni not be brought to see her birth parents, and since she had physical custody of Toni, we honored her demand.

After hours of driving, nearing the designated meeting place, Brittani threw up outside of the car. She was mortified. We reassured her that it was going to be all right and that we would be there for her. We told her that it is completely normal to be sick before such a meeting. Soon after that, we met at their big brother's girlfriend's house.

It was obvious their parents had to have their alcohol in order to follow through with such a meeting. I felt bad for the girls that their parents could not restrain themselves for a few hours, but I also understood the strain and demands on both sides. At least they had shown up. There would be later visits where neither showed, leaving James to search a large city for a relative to visit.

The meeting was uneventful and simple, but in the course of conversation, the mother looked at Brittani and said, "She's Negro," in Spanish. She went on to say, "She looks like her father. She's Negro."

My heart dropped. Brittani twisted her face in the familiar pain. To me, it is not a big deal. We all knew she took after her father and had more of the tight curls of her Puerto Rican father, but I could see that, to her, it was yet another rejection. Rejection she knew all too well. Brittani spoke little about it, but when she did, that is all she remembers. It haunts her still. Chloe was the image of her mother and was admired for that.

During another visit, we obtained Toni's parents' signature for adopting her. We took them to a notary in the city with the paperwork from our lawyer. The prospects of adopting Tonita was dreamy, but what happened next in our lives, would almost destroy that dream.

Craziness Hits Our Home

Every summer, the kids went to a church-based summer camp. We chose different types of camps with different themes for each child so they would not be together. They were able to see each other at the dining hall and walking to their activities. It was something fun we did every summer. Unfortunately, we discovered years later that Drake began his on-going sexual relationship with the developmentally disabled friend at this church camp. James and I mistakenly thought summer camp was a good idea and would create fun childhood memories. We did not realize that camp brought back insurmountable insecurities and fears for our adopted children. Dr. Dobson, a nationally known Christian counselor and author, recommends summer camp. I never thought there would be a problem, because I was there as a camp counselor at the same time as our children were campers.

One particular year was especially devastating and would forever change the dynamics of our family and the hearts of our vulnerable children. Jesslyn, who was 14 years old, was in my camp but wanted to be with Brittani and her friend whom we'd paid to have go with her. Jesslyn was visibly upset by my decision, but I knew that having the three girls together would be disastrous. Brittani would make sure of that. However, in all fairness, it was Brittani's friend, not Jesslyn's.

Jesslyn's cabin counselor began to ask questions and make suggestions. I explained in detail that Jesslyn got along better with her age and younger children, more than the older group, so she would do well in my camp. Her cabin counselor continued to meddle in my decision and completely undermined me by asking Jesslyn what she wanted. These few seemingly harmless words immediately destroyed the intimate relationship that we had built with Jesslyn over the course of five years. A few weeks before camp, I had commented to James that our family was coming together and I felt we were more united than we had ever been.

Many people marveled at how we had united such a diverse group of children into a family and how well they all got along. At doctors' offices, restaurants and stores, strangers frequently complimented the children on their good behavior. I had never been happier. I loved my children, and they were not only adjusting, but rising above their circumstances.

The waves Jesslyn's cabin counselor created caused a rippling effect that eventually deteriorated relationships and destroyed the closeness of our adoptive family. This cabin counselor was unaware of the damage caused by her undermining comments. Any experienced adoptive parents reading this are likely nodding their heads in agreement as we have all experienced family, friends, teachers and pastors who have unwittingly undermined the security of our adoptive children. To the rest of you, trust me this happens. Interestingly, before she blatantly undermined me, Jesslyn's cabin counselor always remarked that we had a beautiful family and what a wonderful job I was doing as a parent. If only she knew what she had done. Why could she not trust me as a parent? One of the major challenges faced by adoptive parents is to effectively and subtly educate those close to the family about their children's underlying fears and insecurities and how innocuous comments can be devastating triggers. Our family looked like it was doing great, but our children were always teetering on the edge of insecurity and despair.

Throughout that week, Jesslyn was at odds with me. She was confused and angry. She continued to participate in the array of activities offered at this camp. She kept her eye on her sister, Brittani, and her best friend with jealousy and anger. Her cabin counselor had told her that she should have had a say in her camp placement and she was seething. Toward the end of the week, we all participated in a Native American ritual called a sweat lodge or prayer lodge.

There were hot rocks in the center of the black tent, and the sun soaked into the blackness of the tent. For the younger children, the leaders did not make it as hot. The idea was to pray to their ancestors and to add prayer for deceased and living loved ones. At this time, I did not acknowledge the difference between what I believed and what this prayer lodge signified. I was enthralled by the Native American culture and experience. Now, I am much more careful with spiritual things than I was then. During this ritual, my daughter Jesslyn had visions of her past sexual abuse and had visions of the perpetrator finding her in her adoptive home and abusing her again. These visions were powerful and vivid, and she began to feel unsafe in our home. Her demeanor changed, and her perception of us, the family and herself changed forever. She went to camp an innocent, but slightly rebellious little girl, and came back a disrespectful, mean-spirited, scared, and traumatized person. We fought to help her find her sanity.

We reached out to a Christian counselor who took Jesslyn under her wing and went through a workbook about surviving abuse. This made her behavior worse. We got no useful feedback and were told by the Christian counselor that she was insightful and brilliant – when nothing was farther from the truth. We fought for a psychiatrist, but it took too long for an appointment. We were able to get a therapist who claimed to know a great deal about trauma and primarily used eye movement exercises to deal with past trauma (EMDR Therapy). However, after weeks of admissions paperwork, the therapist did not want to start anything until well into January because she was leaving for Christmas vacation. Jesslyn destroyed her life during this three- week delay.

I became scared to be with Jesslyn at home. The kids and I remained in public as much as possible in order to stay safe. One elderly man from church unknowingly provided a safe haven when we visited to watch old Ingrid Bergman movies with him. Jesslyn became increasingly violent at home. One day, I desperately drove to a police station and begged a uniformed police officer to tell my daughter not to beat on me. None of them would. They sent me to an overweight, plain-looking woman who mediated domestic disputes. Needless to say, that made things worse.

I had a strong faith and knew that God was more powerful than anything Jesslyn presented. I prayed hard and pressed in closer to God. I called local ministers, but was told that if she did not want prayer and the peace that God had to offer, there was nothing they could do. I knew better, but I could not tap into God's power. Finally, one day, I chased her down outside when she was struggling mentally and fighting physically. I was able to safely restrain her. While restraining her, I talked calmly and prayed quietly. I did not stop praying until she suddenly felt calm. She was no longer tense and she was no longer making any noise. She broke the silence and calmly announced, "I feel clean. I have never felt clean before. I feel clean." I quietly talked to her a bit more and thanked God for this miracle.

Over the next few days, I tried to keep things calm in the house, as well as teaching and preaching about what had happened to Jesslyn. She was happier than I had ever seen her, and she had a calmness I had never seen. I was so happy for her. However, just three days later she was worse than ever - she looked possessed. She would have jumped out a second story window if given the opportunity.

I learned an important lesson during those three days - never cry in front of a hurting child. They generally cannot handle a weak parent. They are weak and need us to be strong. At one point, I went into my room to pray and think and be upset by myself, but I changed my mind and decided to confront Jesslyn, in a loving way with tears in my eyes. I wanted to show her how much I cared about her. As soon as she saw tears in my eyes, she jumped up and started screaming. Thankfully, James was home and was eventually able to calm Jesslyn. I dried my tears and vowed never to cry in front of my insecure children again.

I started waking Jesslyn up a half hour early to read a book about surviving trauma. I thought she would enjoy the one-on-one time alone and hopefully learn some things from the book. I wanted her to understand that she was not crazy, but just a sad, traumatized child. I prayed she would come to grips with her trauma, learn how to survive, and become a stronger and better balanced person. I spoke calmness and survival. I jokingly touched her leg one morning when she was having an attitude about getting up early. I was trying to calmly make a funny comment when she suddenly screamed, "What did you do that for?" In my confusion and underlying fear, I asked her with a shaky voice, what she was talking about. She said, "You punched me. You punched my leg." I was shocked. Later, I learned from a book how traumatized children in crisis are in a fight-or-flight mode and can be hypersensitive to sound and touch. It was a glimpse into how destructive post-traumatic stress disorder (PTSD) can be, and yet most of the professionals ignored Jesslyn's past trauma, even though her trauma tainted her perceptions of us and the world around her.

One evening, James attempted to calm Jesslyn after she became upset with Brittani and Chloe. She started to calm down, but then inexplicably screamed at him, "Why are you yelling at me? Please stop yelling at me!" James had not fluctuated his voice from a calm, sensitive tone. Another time, I hurried into the living room where Jesslyn was screaming. I found her rolling on the floor and holding her head tightly. She was screaming that I had hurt her. She continued to scream that her head was hurt while I scrambled to call a trusted friend who would understand. I was looking for advice because I had no idea what to do. My good friend, who had worked with children in a special education setting and mentally ill adults for years, advised me to stay with her, not worry about injury, and speak calmly. Jesslyn's hypersensitivity continued; gentle or accidental touch was enough to set her off. Another time, I had to call the troopers because Brittani accused Jesslyn of taking her pencil. The situation escalated, and I needed help calming Jesslyn. Brittani and Chloe were naturally gifted at sparking controversy and strife which set off Jesslyn.

Brittani never understood Jesslyn's needs and instability. Her lack of compassion stemmed from her own neediness, jealousy and security issues. Jesslyn's behaviors escalated to the point where a shower became a rushed necessity when I felt safe, and a bubble bath became a luxury of the past. When I showered, Jesslyn would be screaming and threatening by the time I finished.

I read several books about post-traumatic stress disorder and adoptive children transitioning out of foster care. My favorite author was Richard Delaney, Ph.D. I was confident I could help Jesslyn as I kept reading that a family is more valuable to an adopted child than

71

professionals or residential treatment facilities. She was prescribed an antipsychotic medication, which temporarily helped her calm down enough to have some peace. Her insecurity and fears were driving her behaviors. I wanted to understand her and help her through her troubles. James and I did and said everything we could to underscore our love for her.

We sought outside help. Our trusted friend was like a grandmother figure to Jesslyn. She had a calming effect on Jesslyn and would take her as needed. After one visit with this friend, Jesslyn seemed much calmer and at peace when she got home. We all stood around the kitchen with snacks and drinks in our hands, chatting endlessly the way we used to. Suddenly, I saw Jesslyn fading. She fainted to the floor as James caught her. We were scared. We had no idea what had caused her to faint. We immediately called 911. She did not wake up for several minutes, and when she did finally wake up, it was only for a moment before she fainted again. We impatiently waited for the ambulance to arrive at our country home.

At the local hospital, they could not find anything wrong with her, but even as the doctor discussed the discharge plan with us, Jesslyn was continuously waking up and fainting. His back was to her, so the doctor had no idea. I explained that her condition had not changed, and I would not sign the discharge paper. Not wanting an argument or to go against a doctor's orders, James began to sign the discharge papers as I argued with the doctor. As Jesslyn stood up to leave, she fainted. Since the doctor saw this, he agreed that she needed further evaluation.

She was transferred and admitted to another hospital, but all tests came back negative. They explained that her fainting spells were likely stress-induced. In hindsight, she was struggling to be happy in our home and struggling with imagined dangers. The struggle was within her. Doctors cannot diagnose that.

Soon after, we attempted to help Brittani, Chloe, and Toni's older brother Vinito, and his family relocate from the city. We stupidly agreed to let them stay in our home until they found a job and home. We had plenty of space and thought that the country setting would be ideal for their three children, as well as themselves. We were excited to have them with us. We gave them several rooms of our home to set up as their apartment so they would feel welcomed. We stored their excess such as books and bins and dressers in our garage. We paid for their U-Haul. Within a few days, we paid for new tires to replace the inadequate tires on Vinito's junky car. When he thanked me, I hugged him and explained that our greatest desire was to have him in our lives and the cost of the tires was insignificant. I hoped that this would be the beginning of a healthier relationship with Vinito. He had a habit of coming in and out of our girls' lives. We would see him and talk to him regularly for a few months, only to get silence for the next few months, and so it went for several years.

We soon learned (the hard way) that Vinito and his wife were having serious mental health and domestic violence issues. During one of their disputes, Vinito choked his wife until she nearly passed out because she was disrespecting our family. James immediately notified them that they were no longer welcome in our home. James spent the July 4th holiday bringing Vinito's wife to her sister's 250 miles away. We encouraged them to seek separate counseling. Instead of trying to get help, they continued their sick, violent relationship. While at her sister's house, his wife continuously harassed us by phone. Our answering machine was filled with her rude, inappropriate messages. We had to unplug our telephone. Without fail, when I did plug it in, the phone rang, and she was on the other end spewing cruel, crazy words.

Vinito's wife soon found her way back to our area. She set up her enemy camp at a nearby dive motel. She successfully enticed her husband to get back with her; while he initially resisted, she won. Their family of five sat in the motel room day after day for two weeks with little to do. We insisted they borrow a Frisbee, basketball, and some toys for the children. Late one rainy night, I received a phone call from him, asking me to pick him and his family up on a dark side street. His car was being impounded by police for not being registered or insured. We never saw our Frisbee, basketball, toys or new tires again. He made no attempt to get his car back and offered no apologies for our losses. Soon after, they all left for Florida, breaking our girls' hearts again with their illusory promises of staying in their lives. Months and then years went by without hearing from them. Their sporadic correspondence worried the girls tremendously, and the girls lost respect for their brother and his poor, misguided choices. Unfortunately, he had always treated them this way. James and I loved him unconditionally and attempted to be there for him, when we were allowed to be.

Jesslyn finally ended our daily struggle with her post traumatic stress disorder by running away. She disregarded her own safety. She traded in the safety of our home for the dangers of the world. She walked eight miles in the dark on a cold winter night to a local gas station and left on a snowmobile with the first guy who said hello to her. They ended up in a high-speed chase with police.

Jesslyn's escapade ended in an abandoned building in a nearby town. Her new 'friend' claimed to be a carpenter that was fixing the abandoned building. She smoked for the first time in her life and had sex with him. When he was finished with her, probably fearful that he would get caught, he dropped her off to a dark, wet, cold aluminum shed outside of a local snow-cross event. The local police ignored our pleas to find our daughter. They assumed she went with someone she knew and assumed she would be fine, but we knew better. We tried to explain that she did not have the kind of friends that she could walk to and stay with without us knowing.

We begged the police to check the local snow-cross event, but they refused. We begged them to alert the nearby hotel, but they refused. The following evening, we realized that if we wanted to ensure our child's safety, it was up to us to do the police's work.

We spoke to the cashier on duty at the local gas station the night that Jesslyn ran away. The young cashier was angry with herself for not calling the authorities. She thought it was odd that there was a young girl wearing a backpack, shivering in the cold night by the pay phone for a long time, but she did not take the time to question the young girl. We asked the gas station to look at the video to perhaps get a picture of the guy who bought gas and took our daughter, but the video was blurry due to the grease coming up from a deep fryer. We walked around the race track and left a picture at the front desk of the hotel. Late the next night, the hotel personnel called and confirmed our suspicion. Jesslyn had walked in to use the bathroom and seemed to need to clean herself up. We alerted the police, and they did not know what we were talking about; it was a new shift and the information had never been relayed to them. Our struggling daughter was not even safe in a small, quiet, innocent town. When the police arrived, our daughter fought them, but ended up in the police car after the tussle. I begged the police to take the information they had and attempt to find the man who took advantage of Jesslyn's fragile mental condition, but quickly learned that only happens on television.

The next year was difficult for everyone. Jesslyn fought her handcuffs as she travelled to her institution. At the institution, her behavior was incorrigible and crazy enough to have her moved. Another institution took her for a week until they too decided they could not control her behavior. After the fifth move, she settled in, and the group home kept her until she aged out at seventeen years old. We were relieved to hear that the group home had agreed to keep her, because with each move we were accused of abuse. Jesslyn insists that she did not file these abuse allegations but that the group home staff must have done it. It strained our already weakening relationship with Jesslyn, because we were preoccupied with keeping our family safe and intact, rather than addressing her underlying needs. When we visited Jesslyn, we brought her some of her sentimental items. Each time we visited, she was disrespectful and screamed at us for not bringing the right things and mocked us for what we did bring.

Jesslyn was allowed to do as she pleased in the group home. She was given freedoms she was not ready for. She got new clothes, even though her closet at home was full of good clothing. She wore skin tight clothing, showing much of her body, listened to hard rock secular music, added extra piercings, and started smoking cigarettes. She had an older boyfriend who she was able to visit often. When she wanted to go to a party she was not allowed to go to, she ran away, attended the party, and returned afterward. She joined a gang, which led her to a breaking and entry and destruction of property charge. The changes we saw in her saddened us. She had been doing well in our family before her breakdown. I was hoping the group home, staff and professionals in her life would direct her toward us, but they pulled her from us. We could never compete with this newfound (inappropriate/worldly) freedom. She had no interest in treating us with respect or coming home.

Jesslyn treated us the same way at our court appearances. She made a mockery of the courtroom, screaming at me for random items left at home while the arrogant judge ignored any sense that I tried to make of the situation and demanded that Jesslyn get all the items she screamed for.

When I respectfully explained to the judge that the radio Jesslyn is asking for broke years ago, he commented on record, "Well, then, good, you will have no problem giving it to her." As I tried to speak up to explain that we did not keep broken things and that it had been thrown away years ago, he turned away and ignored me.

Her lawyer was more immature and disrespectful toward me than the judge, while they were both overly-friendly with one another. The small-statured, lawyer walked around the court lobby bobbing her body up and down unprofessionally, like a 12 year-old, telling all the court officers how sweet my daughter was and how she would adopt her herself, bellowing that she had an empty nest at home. I could only sit there in disgust - Jesslyn was my daughter. I had not done anything to earn this treatment.

James and I were still part of her life and planned to get her back once she was on medication and had the proper adoption therapy. We had not lost our parental rights, and she was not up for adoption. Ironically, while the lawyer was calling Jesslyn sweet, Jesslyn needed to be handcuffed and shackled to a bench because of her incorrigible behavior. I think they would have gagged her with someone's sock too, if that were legal, because she screamed about everything. I sat helplessly by as the adoptive mother whom they all chose to demonize. I wish that I could have spoken to my daughter civilly and work through the lies and fears, but I knew it was pointless at that point.

Afterwards, I wrote a letter to the State Bar Association about her lawyer's behavior in and out of the courtroom. I hoped that she would be sanctioned because of her unprofessional and inappropriate behavior. She was an embarrassment to her profession. Weeks later, I received a response to my complaint explaining that while her behavior may have been inappropriate, it was not unethical or illegal, and they would not be looking into it any further. It amazes me that if I acted like that and said those things, I would either lose my job as a human services worker or be formally written up. Why are some professionals so well protected?

Years later, I found out that this lawyer had been adopted at a young age. Interestingly, many of the professionals in our lives have been affected by adoption in some way and are biased based on their personal experiences. They randomly insert their emotions and perceptions into our situation without asking to hear our story. Like most of the professionals that we have sought help from, the lawyer probably thought that Jesslyn's behavior was in response to us giving up on her. It could not have been further from the truth. We adopted her when no one else wanted her. We kept her through violent fits of rage that no one else would have put up with, and we stood by her still, hoping to get our wounded child back after she was professionally evaluated and put on the correct medication and therapy.

Throughout our contact with the court, police, case workers, child protective workers, and therapists assumptions were made about our family based on little to no substantial evidence. These assumptions (and lies) are written as fact in their files, counseling records, court papers, and official documents, and there is no way to change it. Their assumptions were repeatedly used against us over the years. There are numerous examples, but I will give a few.

As a fresh beginning after Jesslyn had run away from the runaway shelter, James urged the kids and I to take a trip to the ocean shore to relax, regain our sanity and regain our sense of family unity. On the way there, a court official called me on my cell phone. As I was driving on a traffic-filled bridge in rush hour, he scolded me. Raising his voice, he yelled at me for leaving the state, making me feel like a horrible, uncaring parent, even as I tried to explain what we had been through with Jesslyn and why we chose to take a temporary break. When I told him my husband was left behind to handle things, he calmed down.

Documents stated that I "was unwilling to remain in contact with Jesslyn" in her file. This was a lie. I kept the letters Jesslyn wrote in response to mine, hoping that this statement would be erased by evidence, but no one was interested in the truth. I willingly remained in contact with Jesslyn and prayed that she would be prepared to return home by the treatment professionals. I called her residential treatment facility several times, only to get told she was not available. She was never told by staff that I called. I also spoke with the therapist, the school counselor and the numerous social workers that came and went. I sent letters each week telling her I loved her, giving her updates on life at home, and reminiscing about past memories. I was hoping to bring her back to reality.

At each meeting or conversation with the professionals in Jesslyn's life, they seemed to have one agenda: to make me out to be the bad guy in front of my daughter. Nothing positive was ever written about us. The paperwork stated that I was "short and uncooperative" in my communication with them. This was also a lie. I answered all questions as honestly as I could. I had nothing to hide. I often caught myself on the phone with them for long periods of time, telling the worker more than what they asked. I promptly sent back any paperwork they had me fill out. They did not give me the same courtesy. They relied on background information from our county which had not liked me since I had advocated for the children in my mother's foster home. They also believed our angry, troubled teenager, who was confused by the rejection and insecurity issues of adoption and struggled with post-traumatic stress disorder and attachment disorder.

It was easy for them to believe our angry daughter because the residential treatment facility had erased her attachment disorder and PTSD diagnoses, as if Jesslyn was a chalkboard and her past could be erased. As a result, her therapists did not address the root of her behaviors. Without these diagnoses, we looked like adoptive parents that threw away a sweet adoptive child. Just as troubling was the way they swept all of her behaviors in our home under the rug as if it would never happen again if we all forgot about it. I have read books by experts, who insist on finding the root causes of the behaviors and dealing with the root cause. Her therapist concluded we were the root cause of her behavior problems. This lack of reality based approach did not benefit Jesslyn. We desperately wanted our daughter to get the help she needed and perhaps, even return to us a bit more mended and ready to take on the challenge of living in a family setting. However, this never happened. Years later, Jesslyn told us that her lawyer and case workers regularly told her we did not care about her and did not want her back. All we had left of Drake, and now Jesslyn, were boxes of documents. I saved every correspondence. After every frustrating meeting, phone call, or visit I would feverishly write down every point that I would make, should anyone ever want to listen to reality. It helped me cope with the loss of our children and sordid treatment by professionals. I would continue to write these responses throughout the years to come and accumulate several boxes of documentation.

Another One Bites the Dust

When I thought I could finally take a long sigh of relief following the upheaval with Jesslyn, Miguel went into crisis mode.   Amidst the pain and struggles of losing his sister and multiple abuse allegations Miguel, who thrived on security, realized adoption was not as secure as he had needed or hoped.   I knew how tightly he held onto the need for security, because he would often ask me to tell him his adoption story of how we chose him, what we were thinking, and how it all came together. After the telling of his adoption story, he would begin his machine gun rally of accusations and questions.

"Well, you did not know I called 911 while at a museum for a school field trip," he would say.   I would always reply in the affirmative and he would have a look of shock on his face (as if it was the first time he had ever heard this) and ask incredulously, "And you adopted me anyway?" "Yes," I would reply.

"Well, you did not know I tried smoking when I was living in the last foster home," Miguel said.   I looked into his waiting eyes, and replied confidently, "Yes, I did," to which he asked incredulously, "And you adopted me anyway?" "Yes," I would say.   Then he would come up with three or four more things he did wrong before being adopted by us, that he considered unforgiveable, and I would answer him the same way.   He would end it in awe with nothing more to say until the next time.   Most of the time, he would ask the same questions.

To my complete disbelief, Miguel began to struggle tremendously to hold onto his sanity.   Interestingly, it began with him fainting just like Jesslyn had before her mental health break.   We have always suspected that the stress of insecurity and desire to run caused their fainting spells.

It was heartbreaking to watch Miguel pour over his picture albums I made for him, trying desperately to find the little boy he had lost inside of him.   He could no longer connect with himself or us.   That year was filled with more of the same craziness, but from a sixteen-year-old boy. It was disheartening and frightening. It broke my heart to watch Miguel's rapid decline.

Miguel began to feed on police involvement. He enjoyed intimidating me and stalking me. He became more and more dangerous and angry inside. We were powerless, so we reached out to psychiatrists, counselors, police, and therapists to no avail. His therapist was younger than us, with no children and believed that he was a typical, rebellious teen. It could not have been farther from the truth. They completely missed the mark and refused to listen to my pleas for help. He and I always had a special connection. He would even come to me with guy type problems in life. He was my baby. I loved him dearly and loved his personality. There was no problem with Mom, but Miguel went along with this theme because it took the focus off of his mental health problems and extreme pain inside. In my attempt to show the therapist how different Miguel could become, I risked my life on several occasions to bring him into therapy when he was crazy. For example, during one trip to the therapist Miguel grabbed the steering wheel, threatening to throw our car into a tree or ditch.

In the meantime, we were getting blow after blow from abuse allegations from Jesslyn's different placements. This caused a great deal of stress on our family as a unit. In our attempt to get Jesslyn desperately needed help, we were being targeted. Our children's security was in jeopardy, as well as the potential adoption of Toni. Brittani's and Chloe's resentment of Jesslyn grew. Jesslyn still denies any part in these abuse allegations, blaming her multiple placements for the accusations.

One child protective report, listed a scratch on her arm as the sole accusation of abuse. It would have been humorous had it not been our life, reputation and family at stake. I called and asked how big and how deep this scratch was, but no one was allowed to tell me. I laughed out loud at them. I told them that I was disgusted that a scratch would come through an abuse line while children are being abused in this nation. I explained that I had not seen Jesslyn in two weeks. I had attempted to restrain her from hurting the other children at our home, and she had a thick winter coat on during the restraint, as she'd been planning to run away again. I tried to stop her from leaving, and she began attacking the children, especially the ones trying to call 9-1-1. From there she spent two hours fighting hand cuffs in the back of a police car. I suggested that fighting hand cuffs could have caused the scratch. Even if I had caused the scratch somehow on her arm through a fluffy winter coat, it was not intentional or abusive, but only in response to her stressed state and trying to keep the other children safe. No one could hear the logic in that or any other reality of the situation.

We were also dodging death threats and assault threats in the mail from an unknown friend of Jesslyn's. When I asked her residential facility, they said that they look at incoming and outgoing mail. I was saddened that no one there would take our complaints seriously and confront our daughter regarding these death threats. Now, she is surprised when she lands herself in jail and I do not blame her. For many years, she ran the show and was never told she was in the wrong. Now she is being punished for these same things she used to get away with.

The unannounced visits and inappropriate interrogations by child protective services, haunted our insecure children. They lived in fear every time they heard a car pass our home. When child protective learned Miguel was struggling in a local psychiatric residential facility, they had no compassion for him. They rushed in like wolves smelling blood. When he told me about their unannounced visit, he cried like a baby. It broke my heart. I could not be there to protect him. He expressed his confusion and hatred for what they were doing to him. He acknowledged that he was struggling inside and they did not care. He spent several weeks in the psychiatric facility, but when they tried a medication, his body began to shut down. They were afraid to try another type of drug. When we insisted that there were many types, brands, and doses of prescription medication, the staff accused us of wanting to kill our son. Miguel was discharged soon after that with no safety plan or aftercare plan in place. He had received no therapy or counseling and was on no medications.

Miguel continued his violence and intimidation. There were several times I had to call for police intervention due to Miguel's violence and dangerous actions, only to be told that, due to his age, there was nothing they could do but lecture him. They said he had to be a threat to himself or others. I would not have called the police if he was not a threat to himself or others. No matter what he did, it never seemed to be enough to fit into one of these categories. Miguel got good at looking stable and normal by the time police arrived on the scene. The most memorable event was when Miguel pointed a BB gun at my face, an inch away. As I looked down the barrel of the BB gun, I became sad. I knew Miguel was hurting. I loved him, but could not reach him. I contemplated how much damage a BB gun might do to my eyes, but I was not scared at that point. When he began to hunt down my other children, fear gripped me. I tried to call 911. He came up behind me with the other phone off the hook, taunting "Need this?" as my call would not go through. As he went to find the other children again, I called 911 as fast as I could.

James was at work about 6 miles away at the time of the incident. He was talking to a co-worker, who was wearing a scanner as he was a volunteer fireman, when he heard the police dispatched to our home. My husband immediately left work for home, only to see Miguel standing by the police car when he arrived home. He saw no one else, but the police officer. He feared for our lives. It was never easy these days for him to go to work, knowing what I was going through on a regular basis, but he had to earn a living. Thankfully, James found us all safe.

Miguel was sneaky, deceptive and scary- and loved the power of it all. I tried not to give him that power and I tried to remain calm because I loved him dearly and saw the scared little boy inside of him, but he knew the kids were my biggest concern so he often targeted them. I was trying to ignore the negative and focus on the positive with him. I tried desperately to shelter the others from the trauma he was causing and the chaos and the fear, but it was impossible. I tried desperately to keep them safe from his anger and confusion and sadness, but he always seemed to find where they were hiding from him. He never hurt them physically, but he did threaten and walk around with hatchets, hiding them in the wooded area outside our house, and hit my vehicle with a baseball bat and threw rocks at us. I wanted this craziness to end with Miguel and for the other children to be left unscathed by the trauma. This was not to be the case. The loyalty he felt for a sister whom he never bonded with, was tormenting him. We tried to counsel him through his array of emotions and confusion, but to no avail.

Miguel turned seventeen years-old and we got him his own apartment. We felt that it was our only hope to keep our family safe and help Miguel. We thought that we could parent him from afar, bringing him all of his needs, assuring him that we would continue to care for him, and separate him from the attachment of being in a family. We were praying that this would settle him. His case manager continued to take him out weekly and we visited almost daily. His meals were paid for much like a collegiate meal plan. He was also enrolled in the local high school. We were hoping that it was the closeness of the family that he could not handle, but that with this move, we would be all right. Many people, including his case manager and the school officials, did not like the fact that our son was on his own at seventeen, but they gave us no other options. We fully expected additional trouble with child protective, but we also knew it was our only hope and that he was too dangerous to be left at home. No one else would help us. It tore at my heart every time I read one of those domestic violence signs because no one cares when it is the child intimidating and abusing the parents. When our rental home was empty, we moved Miguel into that. It was a three bedroom, one bath, two-story single-family home.

Miguel seemed to be getting more out of touch with reality and dabbling in evil, but he had a case manager and I brought him to a therapist regularly. No one saw him for who he was, and no one would listen to us as if we were making it all up. The case manager was good for bringing him to the gym to work out which made me nervous as he already flaunted his power and strength. Not long after attending the gym regularly, Miguel had gotten a hold of my wrists and would not loosen his tight grip. The look in his eyes was of a man who would rape to feel the power over the woman. I am sure he saw the worry in my eyes even though I tried desperately to show no concern.

Odd behaviors became his norm. Our role in his life began to be damage control. He would turn our thermostat up to 90 degrees and open all of the windows. We would find odd evil masks in the closets. Food became a huge control factor. Food has always been a control factor for him. As a child, he would steal foods in wrappers and save these wrappers in the pocket of his shirts until we would find up to fifty of them. Now, in his own place, we would find our food mashed onto the ceiling, crusted into the planks of the wood flooring, and molded in the refrigerator. I brought him food daily, homemade, as well as his favorite wrapper and preserved food. It all became a game to him. Our love and compassion became more of a game to him, as well. Our pain and our desires for a better life for him began to fade into his insanity. His angry and hurtful words trumped anything we could do that would be good.

Once James's parents moved into our rental, Miguel began taunting them and showing a complete disrespect for who they were. He stole almost a hundred dollars from them. Amidst the craziness, we had an order of protection put against him. It came to a head one day when he began throwing a bunch of papers out his second-story window and, when asked to pick it all up by his grandfather, Miguel threatened him. James's parents were legitimately scared and locked him out. The case manager put Miguel up in a hotel room. A hotel room for someone who is known to be dangerous and a threat to the well-being of two older defenseless people seemed so backward to me. But why wouldn't it? Everything else seemed to be leaning to the rights of the abusive child, rather than protecting us. James's parents lived in fear.

A couple days later, Miguel was placed in a group home in a nearby city. The group home staff ridiculed us and accused us of not caring about our son. How little these group home workers knew. For example, one worker began harassing me over the telephone about not caring enough about my son to buy him clothes that fit. He went on to say that some of his clothes were so small they would fit a five-year-old.

His disgust with me as a parent hurt me deeply, because I loved Miguel with all my heart. My greatest desire was for Miguel to come to his senses and tell all of these people the truth, but it never happened. Instead, I hung up the telephone and cried. Later that day, my heart sank when I realized what that ignorant group home worker was referring to. He was referring to the clothes that Miguel, as insecure as he was, wanted to keep. There were clothes he refused to allow me to get rid of so we kept them in his drawers. I was so angry with myself for not noticing those precious clothes he loved so dearly and had kept them for him when he became older and perhaps more stable.

After all that Miguel had done to us and our reputations, my heart still broke for him. He was a little child inside. When he left to go to the group home, he brought little with him, but he did bring his teddy bear which he has had since foster care. Now, at a group home with staff and other residents, he could not disclose his childish desire to keep his kid clothes or teddy bear. He had a reputation to uphold, even if that meant making us look bad. I was saddened and disgusted by the staff members' lack of professionalism and knowledge of adopted traumatized children. Miguel's social worker was more than unprofessional. She made assumptions about what was going on, probably listened to some stories Miguel made up, and began verbally attacking our parenting. She also told Miguel that we got a subsidy for taking care of him and he should be getting every bit of that money. This crushed me. James and I purposely never told our children that we got a subsidy because we never wanted them to think that we were getting paid to take care of them, paid to love them, or paid to adopt them. We wanted them to experience a family without the stigmas of foster care and foster care subsidies. There were many times in their lives that I thought of refusing the adoption subsidies, but I also knew that it allowed me to be a stay-at-home mom and give them a childhood they never had. Miguel already suffered from insecurity. This well-meaning social worker compounded it.

On the seventh anniversary of his adoption day, we were sitting in court, being sued by Miguel for his adoption subsidy. We were fearful he would be rewarded the full subsidy and use it for drugs and alcohol.

The group home assured us money gets locked up and used for assigned purposes. We were in communication with Miguel regularly, supplying any needs such as clothes, sneakers, and haircuts. We bought him anything he asked for, as well as bringing him homemade cookies, but the social worker was going to enter in and save the day by telling Miguel he should sue us. In the court proceeding, Miguel admitted that he did not see the need to sue us for the money, but because his lawyer did not want to waste his time, they agreed to a lower amount of $100 a month. Sure enough, that money supplied him with his needed fix of drugs and alcohol, and he soon became an addict. Our fears became real. The group home staff that yelled at us on the telephone and treated us like uncaring parents, unknowingly assisted our son in beginning his drug and alcohol addiction lifestyle.

The pain of this mess, drew me closer to God and His unfailing love. One day, as I was driving, my brain and heart had had enough of the whole mess. I began pouring my heart out to God. As I poured my heart out, I told Him that I did not want to lose my family. I loved my family dearly and I wanted others to see our family, and choose to adopt as well. In my heart, I had always wanted all of the children in foster care to have an adoptive home of their own and to know that someone loved them. As I cried out to him in anguish, pain and complete despair, all while having my eyes on the road driving carefully, He had the word, "PRIDE" written in my eyes straight ahead. I was dismayed and confused so I did what I always do when I do not get it, I began to argue with God. I began to explain that I simply wanted people to see my family and have a heart for adoption. I explained to Him, the Great, Almighty, that in fact, it was not pride that I was falling into. He let me argue my point and cry, and written in my eyes a little larger, was again, the word, "PRIDE" in capital letters. I still disagreed, but learned that He must know what He is talking about so I figured I would consider it to be true, but again, I cried and begged him to save my family. I asked him what we were doing wrong. I begged Him to lead James and I to the right people to help our children, rather than listen to their nonsense. I begged. I pleaded. I wanted to know what we were supposed to do to stop this cycle and this big MESS. Just then, he spoke to my heart and said, "My Hand is in it."

I am an independent Type A personality and a fighter, so I responded with a fight. I am surprised when He ever talks to me, because I always seem to fight with him, but I guess He would rather have honesty than silence. I could not see how this big mess could possibly be something that was supposed to happen - in His plan. I loved my kids, and I did not want to see them go down this ugly road. He replied in the affirmative, "Yes, My Hand is in it. Trust Me."

As difficult as it has been throughout these years that experience with God has held me close to Him. Life does not always look pretty. Life does not always go as planned. Even a noble purpose has to first be surrendered to God, and only then does it become His purpose for you. It often looks messy and does not always go as smoothly as we would like, but it goes the way He wants it to go when we keep Him in it with prayer and supplication. My prayer for all of my children is that they have experiences like these to help them get through life. Unfortunately, even these experiences can be forgotten and lost in the trials of life's circumstances. We cannot let them. We need to remember them, live by them and pass them onto our children.

Amid court dates, death threats and abuse allegations, our love for Toni prompted us to proceed with her adoption. A year after meeting with Toni's birth parents and the year of fighting with CPS allegations of abuse, we were told by an adoption lawyer that the signatures we obtained by her birth parents were not legally binding. They had not had a social worker present to ensure that they understood the ramifications of the surrender. In addition, we should not have been present because it could have been coerced signatures. We worked hard to locate the birth parents in the first place for the original sign off and were not sure if we would ever find them again to sign another set of papers. While we were ducking the blows of the abuse allegations, Toni's father died. They never saw one another before he died. Dedra would not allow Toni to go to the city to see her father, so we'd promised him that after she was adopted, we would bring Toni to see him. We were never able to fulfill that promise. Additionally, it meant that the mother was more difficult to find, but Vinito helped us find the clinic she used in the city and we contacted the social worker there. After a couple months of missed appointments, Toni's mother came into the clinic and willingly signed the updated adoption papers for her to be with us. I was relieved. That stressor was over. I felt relieved for Toni's mother, too, as she did not want Toni living in Dedra's house. She did not trust or like Dedra. Nor did we.

I was excited for the progress with Toni's adoption but my heart went out to Miguel. I envisioned his adoption day and how happy he was. Our lawyer's wife made us a pan of caramel brownies to celebrate our ten-year-old's adoption day. What happened to Miguel's happiness and security? It was an accumulation of things. It was difficult to explain to people who did not understand and did not take the time to understand. Miguel never dealt with the major issues of being horribly abused, rejected, neglected and adopted, or with the losses, turmoil, pain and trauma. He felt stupid because school was too difficult for him, but he was too embarrassed to admit it. Jesslyn demonstrated to him that there is no security in adoption and adoption is not forever. He was also feeling the natural maturation process and preparing for transition as he turned sixteen. The mental health professionals did not point him back in our direction, but directed him away from us. There is a list of major contributing factors to his current lifestyle, but who do we go back to: his case worker, the child protective investigators, his law guardian, or his therapist? Would they care to know where our son is now and how he lives his life because they did not take the time to understand our son? There were many people we asked for help, but they all ignored our pleas.

Currently, he is homeless, living in basements of people's buildings, stealing from parked cars, abusing drugs and begins his days drinking. We paid his rent for a few months, until we found out he was spending the money on drugs and alcohol. He has not accepted or sought the help he needs, but feeds off people's generosity. He is a good-looking con-man. He occasionally lands himself in jail for a few nights or months. I always said I would never visit my child in jail if that was the path they chose, and I have not visited any one of them. James and I may be wrong about that, but it has been something we have stuck with. We have elected to help our children in times of need in other ways, but have never visited them in or bailed them out of jail.

It hurts that he, like many after him, has forgotten the depth and meaning of all the fun we had together as a family. It hurts, too, that he has forgotten and put aside all of the pains and traumas of his childhood with biological family, only for all of that anger and resentment to be placed on adoption. He and Jesslyn were horribly abused in their biological families, causing severe trauma to their young hearts and minds.

My children were becoming files which became boxes of documents. Their paper trail became a work out for a heavy weight champion. I would often stare blankly at those boxes now representing my children in disgust and anger. I was angry at the ignorant professionals that were not capable of seeing the truth and pointing our children back toward their family.

Puberty Hits Hard

Puberty, a change of family dynamics, well-meaning friends and transitions to college life, created the insecurities and jealousies which ultimately destroyed any relationship we thought we had with our older children. Their behaviors, their loyalties, their thought processes and their perceptions reverted back to eight and nine years-olds full of fear, anxiety and rejection. Age fourteen was tumultuous for them, and therefore, for us too. Screaming fits and depression hit like bombs on D-Day. We did not expect them, we did not see them coming, and we did not know what to do about them. We understood them well enough to have a healthy outlook on the root of the problems and most of the time, we combatted these episodes with compassion, listening and reality therapy. Some of the time, I did not.

James was Brittani's sounding board, as she felt closer to the male role models in her life. Chloe was my responsibility, as Chloe was a girly girl and could not relate well to James's direct ways. She needed the drama, emotional outbursts and affectionate responses. I was not dramatic, emotional, or overly-affectionate, but I allowed her to be and understood her ways. James and I were a good tag team, exhausted by the constant trials, but a supportive legion. We rarely fought about differences in disciplining or any other differences for that matter. Years ago, when Drake first began splitting the two of us and making us doubt one another's competence as parents or overseers, we made a conscious verbal pact. These children would not draw us apart, but only draw us closer together. Praise God, we have been through the mud and the mire, but we have been married over 20 years now. It is exciting to realize this milestone normally, but even more so when you have been through so much trauma together. When our children experience trauma, so do we. James and I joke that we both have PTSD (post-traumatic stress disorder) from our children, but if we were tested, I am sure we would test positive for PTSD as well as attachment disorder. We struggle with flashbacks during the day and nightmares that haunt us at night.

One of my favorite memories of Brittani's sudden outbursts is the day that James and I thought it would be fun to take the kids bowling. James had a chiropractic appointment at about 11:30 am, and we planned to all go with him and go bowling afterward. This would run into lunchtime easily. We were careful not to skip meals with our children, as they had all come from such malnourished and neglected backgrounds. So I announced the dilemma and suggested everyone eat a small morsel of food before we leave. I suggested anything from a piece of bread to a full meal, whatever they felt they needed or wanted given the hour of day, their hunger at the time, and their anticipated hunger. I always liked to fully explain ideas to them when the situations were new to them in any way. Brittani did not like surprises or flexible schedules. I tried to cater to that need of knowing what is going on. We would often have family meetings to discuss the day's events ahead of time. After I explained that they should eat a little something, Brittani broke out screaming.

"That is why we are all fat!!! You make us eat when we are not hungry! We do not want to eat, but you are shoving this food down our throat! We should not have to eat if we do not want to! We are fat because you make us eat all the time even when we are not hungry!"

James and I stood there, wanting to laugh at the absurdity of it, but knowing that in her mind, this was real and we could not laugh or we would all die. Our children were never fat growing up, nor did we ever focus on their weight. Our children were always active, trim and some of them, even thin. They rarely watched TV except as a family. Our children always played outside so much, they did not have time to get fat.

We noticed a recurring theme in our children's outbursts and complaints against us: they seemed to attack everything we did right, not what we did wrong. I have plenty of faults and I make more than my share of mistakes parenting, but it was not our faults or mistakes they were complaining about. In response to Brittani's outburst, we attempted to explain again our plans to go bowling and that it would be lunch time and we did not want anyone hungry. Our compromise idea was to bring a sandwich in case they got hungry.

I say "they" when I am speaking about Brittani because anytime one of them had a fit or was depressed, angry, sad or disagreed with something that was said by James, I or the other children, we got the full wrath of both, Brittani and Chloe. They immediately came together as allied troops and their opponents did not have a chance. They would bring out whatever ammunition was needed to defeat their enemy. Most of the time it was psychological warfare, and there was no return fire for that. Ironically, they have no similarities and do not get along. Even now, in their twenties, they fight constantly, live in different states, and gossip about each other.

I would be amiss if I did not mention the time I was grocery shopping and asked Brittani to get a bag of carrots for me while I collected some apples into a bag. She came back with the smallest bag of carrots they offered. I joked about it not being enough to feed our crew of 8 and said, "Get me the big bag. You all like carrots." She was finished. She threw the small bag of carrots back onto the pile, twisted her face up in anger, folded her arms so tight a python could not have done better, and stood, silently. She held that stance, except she walked with the cart, for the remainder of the shopping trip. I was embarrassed because she was fifteen, but there was no longer anything I could do. I tried to lighten it up and allow her to let go of the small mistake, but she would not budge. One thing she has never learned to do is to laugh at herself, and I warned her many times that it makes life easier when we can laugh at ourselves. She never mastered the art, nor did she even attempt to do so.

Every year, after being allowed to go to a week of camp at our church's camp, the girls would come home self-righteous and continuously judge us and spew angry words. Neither James nor I learned our lesson as this went on for four years with the same church insisting that a week of camp could change their lives forever - for the good. Every year, we prayed this would be the year they grasped the love of Christ and living as a Christian. Every year, this anger would last from August camp through the holidays. All in all, we saw the good in our girls and thought that, through our efforts, fortitude and commitment, they would get through this difficult time in their lives, and be able to look back and perhaps even laugh at it.

Thanksgiving was always especially emotional for them and it would be difficult and worthless to ask them to help prepare the Thanksgiving meal. The best Thanksgiving was when I decided I was not going to have 35 choices of appetizers, foods, condiments and entrees. I made it simple with turkey, gravy from a can, mashed potatoes and fried carrots with pumpkin pie for dessert. It was work, but it was not so taxing that I would be resentful that no one would help me. We had a good time eating and enjoying one another that day.

The best Christmas we ever had was when I made the decision that I was not going to buy them anything for Christmas. It sounds terrible, but their attitudes, respect level and behaviors did not warrant hundreds of dollars of wrapped presents under the tree. I understood they were teenagers and confused and angry, but our gift giving was never matched with happiness, surprise or gratefulness at this age. I decided I was not going shopping. James tried to talk me out of it, but the previous year he was able to do that and it was a train wreck. I literally had tears streaming down my face as I unloaded from my shopping spree that night. The kids were in bed and I was doing the usual shopping and wrapping exercise I did every year to make it a welcome surprise for them. My heart was not in it that year, but James encouraged me to do it anyway. My heart ached so bad, I was balling through each step, almost crying at the stores, and that year ended with the same disrespectful, ungrateful attitudes of the preceding year. Well, this particular year, no one was going to talk me out of it. I had made my mind up. It felt right. It was not anger that was driving me, but necessity. My decision was based on reality and love for them. Christmas was going to be back to what it was meant to be before it became so commercialized: about family, love and a savior born in a manger. Christmas was going to revolve around relationships and enjoying one another's company instead of being disappointed that they did not get the gifts they wanted or a sibling got better gifts. My plan was to play the games they already had rather than get more.

Christmas dinner was simple and we did as planned. My mother got them each a few things so they were not without traditional gifts. We also picked names as we always did and shopped for that one person. My gift was a more thoughtful gift than ever before. I put together a collage of pictures of their birth parents and adoptive family and themselves in a frame. I amazed myself at my creativity. Individuals seemed to delight more in watching their person open their gift than opening their own. Individuals seemed happier with what they got rather than looking on to the next gift to open. It was calmer. It was more peaceful and we spent time with each other playing the games they already had stacked away in the playroom.

I recently learned that friends of ours who adopted all of their children, reserve a hotel for Christmas. They do not travel far, but they reserve a room locally. They swim, play games, open gifts, relax, spend time with one another, eat out and read the Christmas story in the Bible. (Luke 2:1-20) In the same way, they take the stress out of the holidays and made it special, but simplified.

Christmas seems to invoke so many different emotions and feelings associated with adoption and family and where they fall in all of it. Their losses and memories of a bad past Christmas relentlessly come to their minds and hearts. Brittani always talked about the beautiful stereo she got for Christmas from her birth mother and father, but within weeks it was sold for drugs. This kind of pain shapes their beliefs and outlook and ultimately their behavior at Christmastime. The two weeks before Thanksgiving to the end of January was always difficult for Brittani. Her attitude and behavior were emotionally charged, and she would sabotage anything we tried to do that was positive or showed our love.

Oddly, Brittani never remembered these outbursts or what they entailed. If I talked about it, she would listen intently as if it was someone else I was talking about. She looked as dumbfounded as I felt about it all. She had no recollection, therefore, had no insight or preventative measures to take. These outbursts seemed to be coming from so deep within her, they meant nothing to her current psyche. Our attempt to love her through them was not enough, but she refused counseling and always had in the past.

Brittani and Chloe have gotten mad because I said I would do the dishes and they did not have to. They have gotten mad at not being allowed to go anywhere or do anything while they have been on soccer teams, basketball teams, traveled overseas with youth groups, traveled to awake overnight activity nights with youth group, weekly youth group meetings, 4H meetings, babysitting jobs, overnight with friends, day trips with friends, traveling extensively with us, prom nights, and whatever else came up.

As an adoptive mom of children who have missed out on so much of their childhood, I always felt that they needed to experience everything and anything. I rarely said no. I wanted them to be kids. I strongly encouraged them not to get jobs until college, because I wanted them to be kids and travel and do what they wanted to do, rather than be tied down to a job with mandatory hours.

We bought them a car to share when they got their license. It was a used car, but it was cute. We always said we would never buy our kids a car. It would be their responsibility, but we thought it would be fun for them to have independence, and still live under our roof with rules and responsibility. We also thought it would help us if they could run errands without using the eight passenger family vehicle.

Trials in the Wilderness

Trials seemed to be our way of life for a few years. The craziness and heartache felt normal after a while. It was more and more difficult for James and me to relate to anyone outside of the craziness. I did not have any desire to talk to people or visit with people. I did not want to go on field trips with my children, which was fine, because with all of the behavior issues, it made it nearly impossible to plan anything. Doctor visits became only necessary if someone became sick, because I could not plan an annual physical, eye exam, hair-cut or any type of fun outing. Anything we did, was when things were calm and we acted spontaneously and had fun. When people were moody and acting crazy, we were homebound. I genuinely love people, so it was difficult to be homebound, especially for behavior problems. Those were the days when I needed people the most, but I would only be judged if I did go anywhere so it was best to hibernate until that bout was over.

Although Jesslyn and Miguel came to James and I as emotionally disturbed children from a severely abusive background, multiple placements and adoption disruptions, we received a great deal of negative attention from government agencies when they became troubled teens. In reality, if these children do well in a home setting, it is a big deal. These poor kids had been neglected, abused, and rejected so many times in their young lives, it is amazing they can function at all in society. Unfortunately, many social services agencies immediately recognize us as a foster/adoptive home due to the different ethnicities of our children. Because they were obviously foster/adoptive children, it was assumed that we could easily abuse them if we got frustrated with their behaviors, because we could not possibly love them as our own.

This has been verbalized by different case workers walking into my home at various times of our lives. It appalls me. I cannot answer for the bond that occurs when a child is biologically born to a woman as I have chosen not to experience that joyous occasion. However, I can attest to the love I have for each child, the moment James and I decide to adopt them into our family. Before they reach our home, we cannot imagine life without them. Like a birthmother dreams of their child growing up to be a fine young woman or man while the child is yet in the womb, an adoptive parent dreams of their adoptive child growing up to be a fine young woman or man while the child is yet in their previous foster home or orphanage. We want what every parent wants for their child, but we are working with damaged hearts, crushed souls, empty eyes, inner rage and sometimes little or no conscience. Perhaps the bond is different, but it can be equally strong, if not stronger in some ways.

It takes extensive planning, effort, time and energy to become an adoptive parent. The adoption process is not at all pleasurable as it makes your life an open book to anyone wanting to look in, and in some cases, empties the bank account and maxes out the credit card. The wait is often times an eternity compared to the nine months of pregnancy. It is a process that can seem daunting. Often times, an adoptive parent comes home with no child at all and feels that emptiness and loss again. Adoptive parents do occasionally cross the line between appropriate discipline and inappropriate discipline and sometimes abuse. There may be multiple reasons for this. Adoptive parents feel alone, misunderstood and judged, sometimes left alone with nowhere to turn and no resources for handling the grossly-unfamiliar behaviors in their adoptive child. Normal discipline does not change these children's outlook, perception, attitude or behavior, leaving the ordinary parent frustrated, confused and angry. The adoptive children, too, judge the adoptive parents often as harshly as the world. Interestingly, they have no idea what a good parent is, because they have never had a parent who has been able to love and care for them properly. What measuring stick are they using?

If the social services system was more family friendly, experienced and educated in the realm of traumatized children, they could point us to where we could get the services we need for our hurting children. It would make sense and would prevent these children from re-entering the foster care system due to disruption. The majority of adoptive parents are not bad people, but confused and frightened people. It is easy for others to judge an adoptive parent, but until they have walked a mile in our shoes, I wish they would not. We found that professionals as well as laymen, had no extensive education or experience with traumatized children.

Throughout all of our situations we have been through with our troubled children, the good children, those not posing a threat or problem in the home, are generally ignored by any program, agency, or friends and relatives. The attention gets focused on the problem and the problem child, rather than the others who are enduring the threats, the insecurities, and the interrogations by heartless agencies, and the life of utter fear they are now expected to live in. They go to bed at night unsure of what will happen in the night or when they get up. During these times, nightmares were common for us all. We would often compare notes in the morning.

We recognized the pattern of focusing our time and energy on the problem child, but were forced to make numerous phone calls, attend court, take them to appointments, and talk to the troubled child and reassuring them of our love. In that respect, we, too were giving the problem child attention while neglecting the others who needed us. This may have exacerbated the situation for us. The good child sees this and sees no value in being the good child. They also do not get the added attention they need in a time of turmoil, confusion and fear. We wished someone would take the children not posing a problem in our home for a fun outing or for an ice cream but no one did.

Dealing with child protective regularly, gave us a clear window into their operations, techniques and belief system. The most important thing that I learned is that we were guilty until proven innocent. If an individual commits murder, the individual is innocent until proven guilty by the court of law, but if an individual is accused of child abuse, no matter how ridiculous the claim is and how lacking the evidence, the individual is guilty until they decide to prove the individual innocent which they typically do not look to do. They look around the house, finding any proof, no matter how small, that there was a line of truth in what the accuser stated. When they find this evidence, they take it and run with it and they stop their investigation. We never hear another word from them. It sickened me that they had that kind of power and abused it regularly. It sickened me that they would willingly destroy a family to get an indicated report of abuse under their belt so that if something else happened, they did not look like the case worker that let it get by. It also sickened me that we had three abuse allegation cases open at the same time, rather than adding it to the original case.

Investigations were handled subjectively rather than objectively. There was no protocol for a thorough investigation. They ended their investigation when they decided they had enough evidence against you, added and subtracted what they chose to as they wrote up their state documents, and continued the investigation as long as they wanted to, despite the 60 day limit. Too much was left to how the case workers felt about you, rather than proof or evidence.

I also learned that a person can cry hysterically and laugh hysterically at the same time. I had no idea this was possible until I dealt with case workers, child protective workers and my daughter Jesslyn's group home social worker all in one room. After our usual circus display in court, I was herded into a conference room with a table full of case workers and her lawyer. The conversation was confusing. It began like this, "Do you want Sue to check out your home so that you can have home visitations with Jesslyn?" Now that may seem a simple question to answer, but I felt it. Anyone who has experienced such a thing knows what I am talking about. I felt tension in the air. I felt that they wanted me to say something so they could all write it down and use it against me. All eyes were on me. The group home social worker who always spoke kindly to both James and I now wore a stoic stone face. She would not look me in the eye. No one was friendly and no one smiled. I knew something was fishy.

I began to get nervous, but kept my cool. I replied with fact by stating that it did not matter what I wanted to do; our daughter Jesslyn was not ready for home visits, and the group home case worker had said that in our last conversation. If the group home case worker did say that in our last conversation, her stone face sure did not show it, nor did her silence. I looked at her for help, but got none. Someone asked me the question again. I said the same answer, perhaps in a slightly different way. This did not make people happy. Apparently, I was playing their game. Now, I knew I was correct. They wanted me to say I did not want Jesslyn back in my home. They wanted me to say an emphatic, "No," and I would not give it to them. During the conversation, I would not give them the answer they wanted, and you could see them shift around, getting frustrated with me and my innocent honesty. I finally asked them if they did not like my answer, and if this was some type of trick question. This angered them and the one closest to me spoke up and said, "It is NOT a trick question."

"Because," I said, "I have answered your question, I do not mind if someone comes into my home, for I have nothing to hide, but I do not understand why you are asking when the group home social worker told me herself that Jesslyn was not at all ready for this step, but if you feel it would be best for Jesslyn then I don't care." I tried to act as confused as I was.

Finally, someone in the group, began attacking my apparent lack of concern by taking my "I don't care" statement out of context. She repeated the statement, "I don't care," and began taunting me about that statement as if to say that I said I did not care about my daughter. I smiled and explained to the attacker and all who joined her, "That is not what I said," and I repeated the words that I used.

Then all of a sudden, someone else jumped on the bandwagon and attacked my positive posture and my smile "in a situation like this."

That is when I slowly and calmly rose to my feet, realizing that I did not have to stay in that room as a prisoner to be attacked verbally by several people in the room at once. I smiled pleasantly and explained that "ever since I was in grade school, my nickname was Smilie because I smile. I smile when I am happy. I smile when I am nervous. I smile when I am bored. I smile to smile, when nothing at all is going on that would make a normal person smile. I smile and now you are attacking who I am," and with that, I took my freedom to walk out and did so quickly all the way to my car. I shook my head for several miles, trying to shake off the craziness of that meeting. I then broke out in hysterical laughter, but realizing the seriousness of the matter and that these people had my daughter in their custody, I began to cry hysterically. I wanted my daughter to get the help she so desperately needed.

I recognized my state of mind and decided not to go home to the other children like that, but to drive to my favorite spot when I am upset: the cemetery where my aunts and other relatives are buried. I sat in front of the gravestones staring at them, crying, telling God how unfair this all was and that these people had us all wrong. I asked him accusingly why we were being persecuted so, and after listing each wrong that was committed against us for Him, I felt Him say, "That happened to me and I was ultimately crucified." After each complaint of how wronged I was, I stopped dead in my tracks, realizing that He indeed was right, but I always came up with another wrong to which he replied with the same thing and on it went until I was speechless. He had experienced as much and even more than I ever have so who am I to complain about my lot in life, my cross that I am asked to carry, my life's troubles.... He did it all first.

A Sticky Situation Gets Goo Gone

With the influx of allegations of abuse and the chaos in our home, we struggled to continue on the track of adopting Toni. Our adoption case sat for months while one abuse case after another opened and closed unfounded. We never got used to seeing the allegations in writing. The stress it all caused was immeasurable. Thankfully, with the hand of God, our allegations ended as Jesslyn finally settled down in a group home that agreed to keep her. Everyone involved with Jesslyn seemed to steer her away from a relationship with us and had no qualms about her disrespect toward us.

Within six months of losing Jesslyn, we lost Miguel. A few short months after that, we welcomed Toni into our home. The summer the allegations all seemed to end, unfounded, we had Toni stay with us for a time, until Dedra called us to have her come home. There was no set time to bring her home and she said we could have her as long as we wanted so we kept her. I spoke to Dedra on the telephone and she said she was worried because she could not get a hold of us. She did not know our phone number or our address after four years of Toni visiting with us. I was sure to give her the information on several occasions. We had also recently issued her papers asking for her approval for us to adopt Toni. I thought it was odd but I also knew she lies to make herself look good. As the conversation continued, she admitted to me that she knew that the right thing to do was to allow Toni to be raised with her biological siblings. When I got off the phone and relayed the message that Toni would soon be ours forever, our whole family was elated. Our lawyer was shocked, given the whole scenario, that this woman voluntarily gave Toni to us to adopt. It had been a sticky situation for a year and-a-half since we had begun to file adoption papers. We had switched lawyers because the case was not going anywhere. We had retained the birth parents' signatures to allow us to adopt Toni twice and we were dealing with Dedra. We had successfully warded off child protective several times. It was definitely a miracle.

I Need Love

It was a miracle. We had custody of the child that Brittani and Chloe had begged for: their little sister. Visits with her for the past four years had gone so well that we expected her to melt into our family. She did not. James and I saw a little girl who was confused and felt the loss of her previous caretaker deeply even though it was not a safe or an ideal place for her. Stories of what went on in that house concerned us. For example, Toni would tell us that the other children in the home would call her "maggot." This hurt Toni to the core. Every child wants to be loved and recognized as special, but a maggot puts a little girl into a place of being not only unwanted, but disgusting. Girls want to be seen as princesses and beautiful and she was being called "a maggot", as well as ugly and fat. When the caretaker was away, which Toni said was often, Toni would be brought to a "beating bed" where she was beaten and whipped by the siblings in that home. She told me she was told by her siblings to jump on a bee's nest and being young, obeyed them. She remembers bees everywhere and getting stung on the lip and then being locked out of the house by her sister. She also remembers beginning visits with us and falling in love with us and our peaceful, fun home. On the other hand, Dedra was the only mother she remembered well and she loved the siblings. All of these mixed emotions of missing the previous family, but not fitting in, caused Toni to act out. She lied about everything, even if she was blatantly caught. She mouthed off if we gave her a chore. The eye doctor diagnosed her with weak eye muscles from watching too much television in her previous home. Toni learned eye exercises which soon became a source of contention and manipulation. She was not the adorable little girl that came to visit so often during the previous four years.

With this disheartening behavior, Brittani and Chloe began to treat her differently. They displayed insane jealousy if I was at all kind to

105

Toni or spoke to her kindly. If I asked her to "please set the table," I was ridiculed by both Brittani and Chloe for favoring her. One day, I was on the phone, and I heard a lot of voices as I was trying to hear what the other person was trying to say to me. I walked into the room of the voices, and quietly lifted my head from the receiver and said, "Hush," putting my finger to my mouth. Immediately, as if a bomb went off, Brittani and Chloe jumped from their seats, got louder, shouted that I was favoring Toni and I liked her better. I did not know what was being said or what was happening. I hushed everyone in the room, not anyone in particular. I did not make eye contact to anyone specific. It was a general "hush" that was said in a firm, but kind tone. When I was finished on the phone, I had no idea what had happened, but I could see the aftermath. It looked and felt like a battlefield. These occurrences happened frequently and without warning, so much so, that I inadvertently, began speaking to Toni differently to avoid being scolded and ridiculed by Brittani and Chloe. I would speak to Toni abruptly, being short and unkind. I avoided being playful with her. Thankfully, it did not take long before I recognized what I was doing. I was appeasing Brittani and Chloe so I would escape their wrath. I was being mean to a young child so I would not be ridiculed by teenagers. They were bullying me. We had a family meeting about what was going on in our home, and I stopped being intimidated and began helping Toni feel comfortable in her new family.

Brittani's and Chloe's behaviors worsened. Chloe fell into a depression she described as "losing her joy" and Brittani became meaner. It seemed as if Brittani tried to be in a bad mood daily. She hid herself in her room for hours, and when she would come out, she would be verbally abusive, slam doors, and scream often. Ironically, she accused me of screaming too much, when complaining to friends and relatives outside our family. They would blow up at the smallest things. For example, none of us, were ever allowed to touch or to read a book that Brittani had ever read, whether it was a book at home or from the library. Thankfully, Chloe asked to go to public school for high school and we gladly agreed. We had home schooled each child and recognized the fruit of it. It also allowed them to bond more closely to us than a full day of public school. However, to give us peace, we were excited about Chloe's transition to high school. We were hoping that being separated for a few hours a day, would calm Brittani and Chloe down, as they did not seem good for each other. If one was down the other would drag them farther down, rather than lifting them up. I always found this to be strange. In a loving relationship, if one person saw that the other was depressed, the other would naturally uplift the one depressed by reassuring him or her that everything was going to be all right. For example, when I was growing up, if my sister was upset and crying that Mom and Dad did not love her, I would reassure her that indeed they loved her and point out ways that they showed they loved her. So this was foreign to me; the way they would drag each other down. Years later, this would be held against us, that we tried to keep them separate even though it was Chloe's idea to attend public school. Brittani tried public school for two weeks and begged us to let her come back home. In that two weeks, she got all A's and hundreds on all of her tests, but she wanted desperately to be home with us so we let her.

We considered pursuing counseling but they refused to talk to a counselor. We did not think of medication because we thought it was situational depression and typical adoptive issues intermingling with typical teenage attitudes and thought patterns. Because they never expressed a desire to hurt themselves, I did not recognize the need for medication. If I had mentioned it, I am 99 percent sure they would have refused to follow through on that, given their mental states and insight. Thankfully, we were able to help Chloe through her depression and I was so happy to see her smiling again, but with Brittani's overpowering personality and mothering of Chloe, Brittani tended to dictate the family mood and Chloe's attitude toward us. To make matters more complicated, when Brittani and Chloe were doing well, they were respectful, helpful, compliant, kind and bonded. We thought we could help them through their bad times.

Chloe enjoyed the drama high school had to offer. She came home crying often, and I would hold her and listen and offer any advice or reassurance I could. Although I was not brought up with hugging, holding, and affection, I knew my parents loved me so Chloe and I had an ongoing joke that she was teaching me to be affectionate. I would first say, flatly, "So, am I supposed to care?" Then she would explain to me calmly that, "Yes, you are my mom, and you are supposed to care." And then she would show me how to be affectionate and teach me how to hug her and tell me appropriate things to say to her. It was fun and broke the ice many times with sadness and emotions that seemed so large at the time, but smaller as we laughed and joked. She always had such a good sense of humor and she could laugh at herself when needed, unlike Brittani.

The meanness of the two sisters continued throughout Toni's life until Toni was invited to Brittani's wedding. Twelve years later, Brittani wanted her beautiful younger sister, Toni to be a trophy at her wedding. I felt pity for Toni because she wanted to be loved. She wanted to be considered and treated like Brittani and Chloe's sister, but she was only their half-sister and continuously treated as such. Throughout the twelve years, we encouraged them to bond with one another as sisters and to appreciate one another as sisters. Brittani's wedding reception was made up of people she never forgave and never liked, instead of the only two people in her life that have loved her for who she was and stuck with her through her screaming fits, anger and teenage confusion. James was forced to humbly sit in the car and eat a Burger King meal during the wedding reception of his daughter, as he had driven Toni four hours to be at her celebration, at a last minute's notice. Their older brother Vinito flew in for the celebration and my heart ached. Brittani had no respect for him, but only wanted him there as another trophy. He was a good looking guy and blood-related to her. That was the extent of her love for him. I loved him dearly and I hated to see him used like that, but because we always insisted on respecting him and talking to him decently, he never knew how much they did not like him or respect him. The foster mother, too, went to Brittani's wedding. She did not have fond memories of living there as a foster child and often complained about the difficulties there, but again, we insisted on the girls keeping in touch with her, updating her, and respecting her. Chloe adored her because she treated her like a queen and babied her. Under the surface, Brittani and Chloe did not like each other either. They were two different people with different viewpoints and different personalities. They had no common ground except to gang up on other people, and they did that well.

Until a person sees clearly, they do not know how skewed their vision is. I know this to be true. When I went to the eye doctor, I did not know I was in dire need of glasses. At the end of the exam, my eye doctor, put a machine with glass in it in front of me and said, "This will be your prescription. This is what you are supposed to be seeing." When I looked in there and saw how clearly the eye chart looked and what I was supposed to be seeing, compared to what I was seeing, I could not talk. I laughed, a nervous, stupid, uncontrollable laugh. I was so embarrassed, but I could not stop. While driving home for the first time with my new glasses, I kept saying, "Wow, I can see that road sign," and "Wow, you guys can see that?" I was amazed at how clear the leaves were on the trees. I was elated to be seeing so clearly. I was so happy to have had an eye doctor who recognized that I had eye problems and was kind enough to fix them. In the same way, James and I would try to help our children see things more clearly, but with outsiders who would believe their perception of things and outsiders who continuously undermined us, we could never make solid ground last long.

Their perceptions of the world are difficult to convey to those who are not able to compare truth and reality with their misconceptions. One of their most hurtful beliefs that they hold true to and spread to anyone who will listen to them, is that we are not the people who we claim to be. They say that we are fake and that anything that we have ever done that has been good, has been to cover up who we really are. How do you combat that kind of rumor spread against you? These hurtful comments put doubt into our closest of friends. No one knows what happens behind closed doors, so it was difficult to counteract. James and I have spent more than four decades to build a reputation that we can be proud of and can live with, only to have it completely trashed by hurting resentful children.

I have gone out in ice storms to bring homemade applesauce to a dying man only able to suck down soft foods. I have brought my daughters to the orthodontist because a rubber band is too tight, while I am urinating blood but unable to make a doctor's appointment for myself. James and I have spent many hours gutting the upstairs of a house for a fellow classmate James met at law school who needed to make an apartment to help him pay for his house. The children helped too, hoping that they would learn to be unselfishly giving. The children and I have also spent days clearing and cleaning a house for a hoarder where there was barely a path through her home. I took her clothes to the Laundromat, only to find large feces in the washer from her dog who could not always get outside. We live our lives for others, and always have. To have that not only destroyed, but mischaracterized as a cover up, is devastating. We do not do these good deeds for rewards here on earth nor do we always expect a thank you, but we certainly did not expect this treatment.

James has spent hours listening to and talking to our daughters in the night getting little to no sleep for work the next day or a big test for law school. James's demeanor and natural ability to unravel lies and twisted thinking, made him the perfect candidate to tackle the girls' lack of logic, twisted thinking and perceptions. He was good at it and rarely shared with me the hurtful, cruel things that the girls said, so that I would be able to move on and parent according to their needs and desires, rather than be tainted by their cruel perceptions of me and the world around them. They never saw good in anything, only negative. At times, it left him bothered into the night, trying desperately to hold onto reality and Godly wisdom and love for these girls. At times, it was me, who had the pointed discussions with the children. I remember clearly one afternoon with Jadin. His behavior and actions were getting out of control, and I knew it was time to address it with compassion, but sternness, and a demand for respect and change on his behalf. I sat him in the living room and hounded him like an investigator looking for the truth. I was both the good cop and the bad cop. Later on, Jadin reported that when I addressed him, he was not trying to be disrespectful, but he simply could not look at me. He went on to explain that "it was as if I was looking right through him" and he physically could not look into my eyes. Thankfully, his behavior changed and he became the happy young man he always was.

James and I have traveled hundreds of miles out of our way, to help the girls develop a relationship with a brother (Vinito) whom they would never have gotten to know otherwise. One of my favorite surprises was when we paid for him to come up by train and James picked him up after work on a Friday. We had him wait in the back room and nonchalantly come walking in, to surprise his unsuspecting little sisters. They had no idea we had planned it. They were dumbfounded and excited to see him. We also planned a camping trip at James's aunt's house who lived four hours closer to the city than we did. James surprised the three girls by picking up their brother in the city, for the weekend. We had a blast camping out that weekend and throwing spaghetti into each other's tent. We took spontaneous trips to visit him and go out to eat with him. We wanted to show the girls that although there were hundreds of miles between them, they could still have a relationship. They have no understanding of our sacrifices or unselfishness for them and do not appreciate all that we did for them.

Hurtful comments destroy reputations, friendships, and our relationship with our children, but it is the belief system in which they live by and adhere to that cuts the deepest. That is what deeply concerns us. For example, Brittani could not handle anyone who had a difference of opinion, surprises, anyone who did something a different way than she would have done it, or doing something without knowing exactly how to do it. In kindergarten, her teachers reported that she refused to do her work because she did not know how to do it. In her senior year, she was no different, regardless of us trying to work with her on this issue for several years. Her need for perfectionism quickly turned to self-righteousness as she grew up; however, we saw beyond that. We saw a hurting child that feels like she needs to be perfect for people to love her. She is a mess inside and cannot allow people to see that or to help her unravel the mess that people in her past have made. She stays far away from anyone who is willing to stand up for what is real and what is true. In her mid-twenties, she continues to focus on the bad in our home, ignoring any remnant of good. Our troubled children have caused us to lose our friends, church families, financial stability, retirement money, dream home and life.

On Death Row

At some point in this chaos and constant strife, I became increasingly convinced I was going to die young like several of my aunts. It still amazes me how we can convince ourselves of things and become depressed, but apparently God had other plans because I am alive enough to write this book. One of my aunts died at age 32 with two small children. These children, now adults, long to remember what their mother looked like, smelled like, acted like, and felt like holding them close to her. I wish I could help them, but I was too young to remember her either, even though according to my mother I was one of her favorite people. She adored me. Even though I wet the bed as a child, she wanted to have me overnight. Another aunt was married and served as a missionary in the Philippines, but never had children. She died at age 42, but to me, she always seemed so much younger at her time of death, probably because I was born after she died, and she had no children of her own. My father brags that children in the Philippines and the U.S. flocked to her and respected her. She was also an opera singer. I always felt close to her, though I never knew her. These are the aunt's gravestones I enjoy visiting when I am upset. I feel closer to God in cemeteries, especially in front of their gravestones.

My reasoning for being chosen to die young made sense to me. God was not allowing James and me to adopt a baby so that the baby would not be left without a mother at a young age like my aunt's children. I also started having physical problems due to the high stress in the home, so I assumed that was going to kill me. I have heard of stress being a number one killer. Stress causes all types of major problems. I had also reasoned that half of my children were gone due to behavior problems and adoptive issues, so that would leave James with an easier job at home without me.

113

To some people, this might seem trivial or of little consequence, but at this point in my life, it was real, much like the reality our children make up due to their past traumas. This reality became my reality. It all made sense to me, and I had logical proof to back it up. Our children do this same thing with their belief systems. It is as if they have glasses on to help them see clearer. The glasses are adoption, and it is meant to help them view the world in a better light and, at the very least, know that someone loves them and cares about them. However, on these glasses, there are big spots of mud and greasy-type substances. In some places, the glasses are cracked a little. These mud spots and greasy substances are from the abuse, neglect and abandonment. The cracks are the scars these abuses have caused. They can see and so many people think that they are seeing perfectly, but people who know them well and know their realities, know that they are not seeing clearly. Their perceptions of their adoptive parents, circumstances and situations are skewed to the point of being wrong altogether. There have been many instances when we have read parts of our children's diaries, for example. In their diaries, where there should be exciting news of travels, sights and fun, there are redundant complaints, laments, and anger.

Our Little Ones

James and I still desired to adopt a baby. Private agencies closed us as an adoptive home due to being bad-mouthed by the county. The county had closed us as an adoptive home because they labeled us as uncooperative. In the fair hearing, to re-open our home for adoptions, the director of social services admitted that every single thing that James and I did was cooperative, but then she would end with the label of uncooperative. How do you put cooperative, cooperative, cooperative, cooperative and cooperative together and get uncooperative? In school, if I got all A's, my overall grade was an A, but not so in the social services system. The fair hearing was anything but fair. I was hounded for sixteen hours by the county attorney whose only job is to hound foster/adoptive families. I answered every question to the best of my ability. I was given an opportunity to ask questions and present my case at 5pm on the second day of court hearings (a month apart) with a sniffling and sneezing judge. My compassion got the best of me, and I could not prolong this court proceeding. It haunts me still, that I did not do well presenting my case that James and I spent so many hours preparing, but in my defense, I had not realized how formal this 'informal' fair hearing was going to be, and I was no match for a full-time, well-greased attorney. He postured himself to win by ridicule and intimidation. It became obvious that they were not looking for truth and justice, but vengeance and justification for their excessive absolutes. I would be their trophy if they could get me. They had a file on me as high as the ceiling with an array of the letters I had written begging for help for my children. It did not matter who I had written to for help, they had a copy of the letter. They had copies of all of my letters to the editor, the state and congressmen. If they do not like the fact that you speak up against them, and I did often, then they could make up a word to define you for life. My name had become "Uncooperative," no matter how cooperative, humble, courteous and professional I tried to be. My heart ached to pursue my dream of adopting, but moreover I cared about the children. I wrote many pointed letters to the editor because every time I tried to find someone with sense in the county, state or federal position of power that would see how ridiculous the allegations of abuse were, how we were being treated or begging for help for our troubled children, there was never any accountability.

We lost the fair hearing and were permanently black-listed by the county – closed for good. Soon after, our home study social worker, not affiliated with the county, told us of a family that was adopting internationally, without a U.S. agency. She said that the couple had not yet gotten a child so she did not know if it would work out for us, but if we wanted to try, she would help us. We agreed and immediately began the paperwork. The social worker was not the liaison for this adoption; all of the paperwork and legwork was laid on me as James worked full time. It was an independent adoption with no agency. I was ready for the challenge and went right to work preparing the documents.

I quickly learned that some people either do not agree with overseas adoption or do not want to do their job. Whatever the case, it was not easy to get the requested documents. Each document put together makes up the dossier to prove who we are and what our qualifications are to adopt and raise a child from another country. One local bank employee absolutely refused to supply me with the necessary document for my dossier. It needed to be a document that stated our address according to our bank statements and records. She kept saying that she could not prove that we lived there. I tried several different ways to explain that it was only one piece of paper out of many that would be put together in a dossier. She absolutely refused. I died inside. The idea came to me to go to another branch of the same bank. Thankfully, that person was willing to help me out and provide me with anything I needed without charging me. Finally, after much diligence and perseverance, the dossier was complete, the home study was complete, and our immigration electronic fingerprints were done. I never knew how much my fingerprints were worth until I had them done through the government.

Apparently my fingers use up a lot of ink in those digital prints because I went broke paying for James and me to finish this last task – over $1400.

The time came to choose the child or children we wanted to adopt. Our home study social worker thought we would choose a baby, as we had been trying to adopt a baby for several years now, but for some reason, James did not feel led to adopt a baby. James and I decided to request two boys, ages five and younger. Soon, we received a picture of a five-year-old boy and a two-year-old boy. James told me to commit to these two boys. I was more apprehensive. I was nervous. I was worried that they were not the ones for us. I could not feel a peace about it, only an odd combination of fear and suppressed excitement. I was concerned that they did not give us a choice of children to adopt from. I was not normally the worrying type, but this adoption made me worry. International adoption was new to us.

Many years ago, I had looked down on people that adopted from overseas. I felt that there were enough children in the United States that needed a family and needed to know someone cared about them. Now, years later, here I was, in the process of doing something I always disagreed with. The county, despite actively advertising for foster and adoptive parents, closed our perfectly good adoptive home. They were known to close as many foster/adoptive homes as they opened each year.

We used the profit from the sale of our rental property to fund these private adoptions. We took a risk and sent the money to a third-world orphanage not knowing if it was going to produce the two children in the photo or we would be once again, heartbroken. We prayed and we prayed. Our hopes were high. Working with a third world country and its government officials with a liaison to communicate through, was stressful, but eight months after committing to our boys, we received the phone call we had been waiting for. The boys' visas were ready and we could come pick them up.

James and I were prepared in a few short days. James was to fly to pick up our boys alone, and I was to stay with our other children. I was riddled with jealousy, but knew it was the right decision. I was also a nervous wreck. When James left, I cleaned more than I had ever cleaned in my life. I paced more than I had ever paced in my life and I begged people to pray for safe travels and for me to calm down. Deep down, I felt like this could never happen. James and I were never going to get the opportunity to adopt young boys. I also felt that this might be when James dies, going to pick up our adopted children. I had all sorts of emotions, feelings, visions and thoughts going through my head. I was scared and did not believe I deserved to be happy. I had been treated so poorly by my older children, I did not feel happiness was for me. This adoption felt too good to be true. I was not normally a negative, despondent, or anxious person, but apparently, this emotional stress was difficult for me to keep a cap on.

The flight was an 18-hour flight and included layovers. It was certainly the longest trip James or I had ever been on, although I did not take that trip until three years later. James arrived safely, but immediately felt the chaos of the airport and the dishonesty of the people. He was not scared, but was on high alert. He could feel the tension of the war that had ended years ago. He was in an impoverished country. He stood out. After driving from the airport, he arrived at the guest house of the orphanage at about 8 pm on the youngest boy's third birthday. Soon after arriving, he was given our little boys. They videotaped the awkward meeting of an adoptive father excited to meet two scared little orphanage boys. The boys did not know what to do or say. Their eyes were dull with fear. They wore the clothes we had sent with another father picking up his girls six months before. On their backs were their personal back packs that we had bought for the airplane trip home. The back packs seemed to be bigger than their little malnourished bodies. They would not smile, but only frown and stare wide-eyed. The orphanage director attempted to direct them on what to do and say. They gave their new father a hand shake and a hug.

James called me at home when he arrived at the guest house. He joyfully told me that he had his two boys with him. I was speechless and numb. I was seething with jealousy. I wanted to hold our boys and look into their eyes. I did not know what to say. I must have sounded dumb when all I could do is ask, "Do you like them?" James has good discernment when he meets people: what kind of people they are, if they can be trusted, and if they are good people. I was trying to ask how he felt in regards to his discernment about the boys, but no words would come out. I was wrought with emotion. I was not thinking clearly nor in my right mind. I wanted them home. James answered with an understanding tone, "Yes, I like them very much and they are doing well."

Hours later, these two shy, fearful boys were jumping on the guest house beds in excitement, rubbing hand sanitizer all over their bald heads to feel the coolness in a hot climate. James gave them balloons to play with that kept them from going to sleep. Eventually, they fell asleep due to all of the excessive excitement of the day. The youngest boy had a fitful sleep as he had some type of respiratory infection. James feared for his life.

James only stayed for five days, but he went on many road trips to visit people, to see the school the orphanage sponsored, and to relax at a picnic on the beach. Bodyguards took them everywhere and chased people off if they did not seem safe. A group of men entertained the adoptive group with songs; mostly American songs. Some of the group waded in the water of the vast ocean. The waves hit harder on this side of the ocean, than in America. The children did not know how to swim, as most people were taught to be afraid of the water by superstition. The bodyguards remained alert and swooped a child up if they seemed to have fallen or lost their footing.

There was no requirement at that time for a minimum stay, and we were anxious to bring our boys to their new home in America. At the airport, the adoptive father in front of James was told he needed to pay money to get the fourth passport back as they only gave him three. The adoptive father gave the dishonest worker a five-dollar bill. Five dollars was equivalent to five full days of work for most natives. When James gave the same man his passports for himself and our two boys, he got only two back. James immediately noticed he was missing a passport and demanded it back. They tried to act like they did not know what he was talking about in the hopes that they would get some cash out of the deal, but James held fast, demanding his last passport. The man handed it back with no explanation or apology. As James began to proceed in the milling of the airport, a man approached him and accused him of "stealing his little brothers," but immediately retracted his statement and thanked James for helping these little boys. He remarked on how unsafe it is here for children and the good thing that James was doing. He thanked him again and walked away.

The flight was rather uneventful. Samuel, the younger boy, slept the entire flight except when food came. No one had to wake him. He knew when it was time to eat. He cleared his plate each time he was given any food or drink. He loved to eat, and almost eight years later, he still loves to eat, especially when he is stressed. When I traveled to his homeland three years later, he never stopped eating the entire time I was gone. We always tell him he had better stay active if he is going to continue to eat like that. At age three, he remembered one thing of the orphanage: he remembered having his food stolen from him by the bigger children. He was not going to have this airline food stolen from him. He ate it as quickly as he received it. Both Josh and Samuel were well-behaved, presenting no behavior problems. They sat, ate, slept and watched the movies on the movie screens. I know fear must have been writhing inside of them. Everything was so new to them, including their father, and they had no say in the matter.

Meanwhile, in America, I was connecting with an off-duty taxi driver to take me from James's aunt's house where I left the other four children, Brittani, Chloe, Toni and Jadin. He drove me to the Port of Entry airport to pick up my husband and my new little boys. I was beside myself with excitement. I wanted so badly to like them. I wanted so badly for them to like me. On the other hand, I knew that it would take time for them to get to know me and begin to like me. The taxi driver, Jim and I, searched the airport signs to be sure we were waiting in the right place, when all of a sudden, I saw their shoes. We had sent them sneakers for the trip home to America. I recognized the sneakers I bought. I took a picture of them walking on American soil. My heart was beating so hard, I thought perhaps everyone could hear it over the din of the crowd.

The little one, Samuel, would not look at me or smile. I did not blame him. He did not know me, but years later, I could pick on him about this. That same boy is now a mama's boy. The older boy, Josh, was more pleasantly shy. He did not seem to mind the newness as much as the young guy. He willingly took a picture beside me, drawing in little Samuel. Josh looked like a tiny young man with a bright white smile. Samuel was a tiny little boy, reserving his smile for later use. He had a short, chubby stature with a beautiful high- pitched voice when he spoke. He was so tiny, he was easy to pick up. I did not pick him up for a while, as I knew he did not know me and I did not want to begin our relationship on the wrong foot by startling him.

Being put into car seats in the taxi driver's vehicle, the boys looked terrified. To their unexpected delight, the taxi driver's wife sent along with him a stuffed animal for each child so that they would feel more at ease on the trip to James's aunt's house. I was mad at myself for not thinking of something like that, but my mind had not been working properly for a week or more due to all the excitement and fear. I was glad that she had thought of such a wonderful gesture. The children clung to the animals tightly and sat silently for the hour and-a-half ride. They looked with wide eyes as we traveled until at last, we arrived. It seemed like forever. I was anxious to begin our life together with our new boys.

The meeting with James's aunt and the other children, soon to be known as their siblings, was quiet, awkward and sad in a sense. I could not help but think of their loss and their fear and their parents' sadness at losing these adorable young boys, but James reassured me that, this war-torn, poverty-stricken country was not a place for young children. As a matter of fact, a man from another war-torn country had approached us on the bus at the airport, thanking us for adopting the two boys. He said, with tears rolling down his face, that he knows first-hand what it is like to grow up in a situation much like the one we were bringing these two boys out of, and with that, he turned away with tears streaming down his cheeks and walked slowly, as if he had more to say, but could not. I held onto that thought as I raised these two young boys to slowly comprehend the meaning of adoption for them and what these men had been saying when they thanked James on his way out of this war-torn country.

Our Little Melting Pot

Our family was the melting pot for Josh and Samuel. African little ones joining Hispanic teenagers with African American and Caucasian older children. I understand it is not ideal that children are not raised by their birth parents, but where that is not possible, I believe that a uniquely-blended family can make all the difference to a child in need of the love and safety of a family. As a family, we incorporate their differences, their individuality, their ethnicities, and their similarities. We celebrate their differences without making them embarrassed or putting too much emphasis on them. We also celebrate the fact that they were adopted without putting it in their face regularly. We kept the lines of communication open to all of it.

Every day was filled with joy for me as I watched our newest little ones play. During their naps, I missed them dearly. I hated to put them down for bed at night. I could not wait until they got up, so I could watch them some more. I was mesmerized. It was as if I was finally happy and complete for the first time in my life. I was not being treated like a second-class citizen by them in my home like the older girls often had. Brittani stated that it was difficult to be in a bad mood with those two boys around. I was glad because a bad mood seemed to be her norm, but Josh and Samuel's presence slowed her down. The two boys had a joy I had never seen before. It surprised me, especially being from a third-world country, being malnourished and coming from such poverty. They laughed. They played. They smiled. Everyone loved them. Our family was melting together one more time. I was content.

As one could fathom, it was fun to introduce our new boys, Josh and Samuel, to American life. Everything was met with wide eyes and curiosity. Some things shocked them, some things scared them, and on some things Josh and Samuel just took our word for it. Automatic doors were entertainment to them for nearly 30 minutes as I stood in line at the physician's office the day after they arrived. I loved watching their complete amazement. The car windows were another source of entertainment. While I was sitting at a stop light one day, I began to put down the back windows with little to no movement from me. I then told the boys not to put the windows down. They could barely speak. Their eyes were wide and their mouths gaped open.

"We didn't touch them," Josh and Samuel squeaked out almost simultaneously.

I played with the windows a little more until Josh saw through the seats that my hand was pulling the lever. He shrieked with laughter and explained it to Samuel whom also had a great sense of humor about it.

I tried to decrease the amount of newness by making them meals they ate at the guest house before getting on an airplane for America. Their first morning in America, I made hot dogs and rice which was called sausage and rice in their homeland. Samuel would inspect every meal before eating it.

The first hamburger I made him, he lifted the bun, looked up at me with a puzzled twisted face, and said, "A leaf?"

I said, "Yes, now eat it," and he did with no other discussion or problem.

Coming from malnutrition, I wanted to squeeze in as much nutrition as possible without scaring them with too many vegetables and greenery. No matter how much we tried to make them feel at home, we continually made cultural mistakes. When they were chilled one evening, I proudly got them homemade flannel robes to put on. Josh obediently put it on, but immediately had a distasteful look on his face. His pout became a deep depression within minutes. No one knew why Josh was acting so despondent until he finally pointed to the robe he was wearing and said, almost crying, "A dress?" When we laughed, he seemed to take offense, so we put it away for later, when he was more accustomed to American ways.

Samuel refused to take care of his hair with hair moisturizer and oils. I bought many different types, but he would not consistently take proper care of his hair. One day, he was in the beauty store with me and pointed to a container with a man's face on it and asked excitedly, "Can I get this one?" I knew immediately, given their manly culture, why he wanted that one and agreed. Several years later, he is still sensitive to having manly hygiene products.

To make the boys feel comfortable, I also incorporated some of their vocabulary they would use such as "Jook" for poke or pinch or hurt. They called a cookie a "biscuit" and the toilet was a "commode." Any type of sauces, whether it was a cheese sauce, gravy or spaghetti sauce, the boys called 'soup'.

My absolute favorite was when Samuel would say, "Mama, dottie!" I thought it might be a bit of French or British mixed in with English, but looking back, I think it was a three-year-old trying to say, "Mama, watch me!" Either way, it melted my heart every time he screeched it in his high-pitched voice.

The most difficult was when we asked them a question, and they said, "I didn't." For the longest time, we thought they were saying, "I did it." They spoke quickly and blended their words together, slicing off each word so many words were difficult to understand, but this phrase in particular often landed them in trouble, until we understood our blunder. We still struggle with this phrase and have to make them clarify with a fuller phrase than "I didn't."

Occasionally, Brittani caught herself talking like them when she was with her friends which she thought was funny. We all spoke like them, sometimes by accident and sometimes purposefully. I wanted them to feel normal and not as if everything was new and everything needed to be learned at once.

It was not all fun and games. One day, soon after they joined our family, we took our family to shop at a large electronics store in a nearby city. It was too much for poor little Samuel. He seemed to have flipped a lid. He flopped his body to the floor and screamed louder than I had ever heard a kid scream. We scooped his body up as fast as we could and put him into his car seat, trying to buckle it while he kicked, screamed and fought. He would not listen to any redirection or correction. He did not respond to either love or scolding. It was a long ride home with our eardrums begging for mercy. When we got home, it was as if we had all been to a heavy metal rock concert. Our ears rung with sadness at his cries. James insisted that he apologize to everyone for screaming in their ears all the way home in the car. The little stubborn boy refused. James insisted. Samuel refused. This went on for hours. Finally, Samuel thought better of it and apologized to everyone in our family who had to endure his screams. We learned a lot about overstimulation. We learned later on from Dr. Federici, that we should have stayed home for a few weeks without visitors to allow them to adjust properly. Without that knowledge, we did know enough to do simple things and take life slowly for a while.

It was different dealing with the international issues. Immediate concerns were the vaccinations. I wanted to be sure they had the extra protection that inoculations in the United States gives you. We were told the little guy, Samuel, had almost died when he was younger. We were never told what he had or even if they knew what he had, but we knew his little body may still be a bit weaker than some. Another immediate concern was the ringworm. It scared me to think that someone might catch this contagious, distracting fungal infection. Ringworm does not go away quietly or simply. A year later, we were still treating what looked like ringworm. It was as if it became one with them. It grossed me out and it created so much fear within me - I did not want to tell everyone they had this, but yet I could not bear to be the bearer of ringworm in their families. I struggled inwardly on what the best approach would be. Most of the time, I pulled the person aside and told them to wash their hands because my child had ringworm.

The most glaring difference with the international issues versus the foster care issues was the inner workings of the child. The foster children that we had raised have come with so much baggage - so much hurt and pain from their past, caused by their birth parents and the social services system. The same system that was originally set up to help them, destroyed them. They were taken out of homes they loved dearly and put into homes they did not know, without any more than a sentence of an explanation. Miguel comes to mind with this whole ordeal. This is why he could never believe we chose him. He was in an adoptive home that loved him and wanted him and was in the process of adopting him, but the caseworker did not consider Miguel's heart, when they made the insensitive decision to move him. It was not because the foster/adoptive family was bad, incapable, or disturbing in any way. It was because the foster/adoptive couple did what the caseworker told them to do. The caseworker insisted that they send Miguel to another foster home on weekends to get a break from his behaviors, but when they did, Miguel was taken away from them and so was a piece of their hearts. Miguel was never given an explanation. It does not make sense, but it is how the system manipulates people.

Our children from foster care also came with a sense of entitlement. They seemed to feel that since the world dealt them lemons, the world had to make the lemonade for them and serve it to them with a smile. They deserved and expected. Ironically, they did not feel like they deserved a family that unconditionally loved them. In their twisted perceptions, they seemed to think that (based on many heart felt conversations with our children) their adoptive parents were supposed to be perfect. So many times, in my fury and frustration with the kids' perceptions, words, and actions, I would say to James, "If we were Jesus Himself, we would not be good enough parents" for them.

I would get a knot in my stomach when I saw the advertisement for being a foster parent that said, "You do not have to be perfect, to be a foster parent." It simply did not seem to be true, especially the commercial where the foster mother gave the child an ugly sweater for Christmas; it was often held against us, that we did not get them what they wanted or did not do something right. The older girls told relatives and friends that we controlled what they wore. Our dress code was simple and modest. We did not like the girls wearing anything that showed cleavage, and we wanted the skirts and shorts to cover their rears modestly. We wanted them to understand the use of make-up and hold off using it as it is known to be unhealthy for young people's skin. We also wanted them to understand that make-up should be used to enhance their beauty, which none of them needed, and not to cover themselves up. Chloe began using so much make-up in high school, she resembled an orange-faced clown. Any mistake we made or decision they did not agree with was continually second guessed. Any mistake or decision would be held against us in their hearts and minds forever.

Another big difference between our international children as opposed to the foster children is their respect for adults. In our younger children's homeland, if you do not behave or show respect to adults, there are consequences. Josh has stripes on his back from being beaten and bloodied. Samuel saw dried hot pepper and shrieked with delight that he knew what it was and became sober as he stated, that if he was bad it was put in his eye. I stood with my mouth gaping open, but it was a mere fact of life to him. It was a consistent form of discipline which he knew to expect if he misbehaved. I am not condoning such acts of harsh discipline, but the typical American child's respect level has gone down tremendously the past few years. Children feared and respected their parents' at one time in America. I am glad I did. My parents were my stability in life, and I could gauge my behavior, morals and ethics on their response to them. Our little boys nodded if an adult spoke to them. It was a quick, hard nod. It did not mean yes. It meant that they heard you and respected what you said to them. If we needed an answer, we would have to ask again or wait for that answer. I miss that the most because of course, after a few months in America they lost that automatic response.

Law School at Last

James always knew he would go back to law school someday. He had quit a leading law school at age 21 because he did not feel he fit in the crowd and did not feel he belonged there. He returned to his small hometown community where the majority of his family still lived. He resided with his sister who as a single mother was trying to raise three children. He was a live-in nanny and got a job working with mentally disabled adults. On his first day at work, he met me. He knew at some point, he would return to law school. Sixteen years would pass before he returned.

In the meantime, he earned his Master's Degree in Business at a local college, while working full time and adopting eight children. His jobs throughout the next few years included working with mentally disabled adults, working with mentally ill adults in a residential setting, working from the ground up at a local factory which eventually awarded him a position as a manufacturing engineer manager, and later in life, at the age of 38, James became an attorney. I believe these steps were not a mistake and helped make him who he is today.

When James announced that it was time to quit his manufacturing engineer manager position and become a law student, it was of no big surprise to me, and I agreed that it was time. We were not ready financially, nor were our children fewer in number. Thankfully, James earned a substantial scholarship to help pay for his costly tuition expenses. He could not work due to the classes being in the day and the amount of work and stress involved with law school.

I offered to work full time at the place where I had been working relief hours occasionally since I graduated college. I worked nights so that the children would not miss me. I left for work when they were in bed and got home when they woke up. It was ideal, except for my sleep. It began to kill me from the inside out. Fortunately, at my job, if my work

129

was done and the residents were not needy that night, I could sleep for a few short hours, waking up to check the house for any mishaps in the night. Unfortunately, this was not enough sleep to live by, but with Brittani having emotional breakdowns again, I was not able to sleep when I got home. Occasionally, I would simply collapse on the couch with the chaotic play of children all around me.

While I was basking in the excitement of having two young boys which was a dream come true, I was also finishing my master's degree in Practical Theology. During the boys' naps and in the evenings after bedtime, I would do the majority of the work needed to accomplish the task of receiving my master's degree. I worked extra hard because I wanted so badly to spend every second with my adorable two little boys and my four older children who always kept me hopping with sports activities, karate classes, field trips for school and youth group activities.

At this time, James also decided to pursue his law degree, so he was working hard at studying for the LSAT which he took seriously, along with working full time. We had a full plate of activities and I had the family I had always dreamed of. Brittani and Chloe had finally calmed down because they said, "It is hard to be grouchy with these little boys in the house." I loved that the boys brought a calmness, an excitement, and a love to the air. The boys brought us all together, through our mutual love of them. I was so happy to see Brittani talking, smiling, and laughing again. She is beautiful when she smiles. I prayed it would continue and these boys could teach her to be more loving and forgiving of others. I prayed that it would teach her how children ought to be raised, rather than the neglect, abuse, rejection and fear she experienced as a youngster.

James's only responsibility was to go to law school, do well, and earn a law degree. It sounds like a focused plan, but for a family like ours and a life like ours, it was not as simple as it sounded. The chaos and stress of Brittani and Chloe made studying and focusing difficult. It was hard for him to study in our home with continuous battles and their miserable attitudes. It was similarly difficult for him to be so far away from home in law school knowing the strife that I was enduring as a disrespected, targeted mom. He was torn, as he was when he was at work, but he was also determined. He was determined to follow his dream and do the type of work he knew God had made him for. I was his cheerleader on the sidelines, reminding him of his dream, of how proud I was of him, and that God would see us through this difficult time.

Financially, we had to live off student loans. We had no substantial income, as my human services job mainly provided us benefits. It was not enough to sustain a large home, large family, two cars, and the adoptions that would take place during law school. James had made the decision that since it was his decision to go to law school, the children's home life should not have to be compromised or changed at all. They would still live the way we always lived on his income. If ever we had a regret, it would be this. We are still paying for this decision to not only live off of student loans, but to allow the children the same lifestyle they were always accustomed to and yet, the three girls not only do not appreciate the sacrifice we made for them, but they have spit at the sacrifices we have made for them.

I encourage all adoptive parents to take care of their finances and be sure to have a good amount of savings and investments. We originally had savings, but we allowed our compassion for our children and their need to experience everything and live life fully to compromise our finances. Also, I know several adoptive parents that have paid several thousands of dollars for therapeutic placements. Adoptive children are generally more costly to raise, as they have more pressing emotional and mental health needs and a higher level of needs than a biological child. We have also made decisions we may not have otherwise made because of our adopted children's needs.

The Stork is Coming

God uses people in our lives, with both good and bad intentions, to accomplish His plan in our lives. He loves it when it looks impossible to us, because it is not impossible to Him and we cannot brag if it was obviously not our works that accomplished it. We tried three different agencies to adopt a newborn baby. I also wrote to abortion clinics. My dream was not to adopt a baby everyone else wanted, but to adopt a baby no one else wanted. I know it sounds odd. Most adoptive parents want a baby, and I am making my children sound like rejects. Unfortunately, society has thrown away my children, all of them, in one way or another, so society in general, has considered each of my children defective. However, James and I do not. We love our children, each of them. We love how we came to meet each of them and how they came to live with us as our sons and daughters. We feel badly that their pasts were not filled with safety, happiness, and grand memories, but we strive to teach each of our children that they can change their stars. (A Knight's Tale movie). They can be whomever they choose to be, regardless of the horrific details of their backgrounds.

God used a woman who responded to one of my letters to the editor regarding the problems with social services. She contacted me because she was going through a tough situation with the social services. She lived in the poor section of a nearby city, was not overly adventurous, and did not have much money, but her child had more video games and toys than I had ever seen in my life. She professed to be a Christian, but I saw some glaring contradictions. Still, I called often, visited when I could, and loved her for who she was.

In our long conversations, I would often lament that there were so many babies born to mothers who did not wish to raise them. It made me sad to watch small children run the streets alone. She would often talk about a friend of hers that felt overwhelmed with the number of children she was raising, as well as their special needs. About three years after we became good friends, she called me and told me that her friend was pregnant and wanted me to adopt her baby. By this time, I had already met this friend, as she had previously asked me to adopt a child of hers before this one was ever born, but changed her mind. She had refused to meet with me, then explained that her boyfriend was giving her a hard time. We were more reserved and matter of fact regarding this second adoption opportunity.

With this potential adoption, I became more excited as time went on, as I tend to be more emotional anyway. James remained in the sidelines, hearing only what I told him of this situation and my time with the birth parents. He was at law school when I met with her or took her to doctor appointments. He was reserved when I jumped for joy at different aspects of the adoption; therefore, he was less disappointed than me when the birth mother did not show up at her doctor's appointment where she had told me to meet her. He was not as enthusiastic when I told him I heard the baby's heart beat or I saw the baby on a monitor screen. He wanted to be happy, but he did not trust that the birth parents were going to go through with it. He wanted to trust them, but he had felt the stabs of disappointments so many times before. It was a rollercoaster of emotions with overwhelming joy and the pit of despair on each spectrum. It was a rollercoaster we could only share with a small number of people. We could not tell our children as their adoptive backgrounds could not handle these rollercoaster rides. Their emotions already spike to tremendous levels. We needed to protect them until the baby was to arrive into this world.

From June to December, James and I made preparations with lawyers. We found a competent, compassionate lawyer for the birth parents while we relied on our trusty adoptive lawyer that we used for our last three adoptions. We paid for both. I brought the birth mother to every doctor appointment too, but there were few. The way she was treated made her reluctant to receive prenatal care. She was sure of her decision to put this baby up for adoption, but was treated with the utmost disrespect from doctors and nurses. They tried to dissuade her from this decision, to the point of being mean to her. Following one of her early pre-natal visits, she left disgusted groaning that "those doctors and nurses are not going to be there for her when she needs a break to take her children for the day. They are not going to be there to help pay for food, braces, and other needs or wants. Where will they be?" She heated up as she spoke, her voice breaking. She was right and the same people dissuading her from putting her child up for adoption, are the same people who complain when people needing assistance from the government to help raise their child, keep having children. Funny how contradictory people can be. She was so disgusted that she would not go back to the doctor until the month she was due – our baby got minimal pre-natal care.

The birthmother remained strong in her position to give her unborn baby to me. At every turn, this birthmother had it tough. She asked for government assistance that a low-income pregnant mother normally receives, to ensure a healthy baby. The government agency declined her assistance because she was putting the baby up for adoption. So that meant that I could not have a healthy baby, but she could?

Another private adoption agency tried to get involved. This agency had a nine-year waiting list when James and I checked into it, and I understand their need for babies, but they were taking a baby that was not theirs. They began bullying the birthmother into having a meeting with them to discuss her options. She kept trying to assert herself by telling them that she already had parents for her baby, but they insisted to the point that she gave in. As she complained about the agency, I wondered if she believed what they were saying. First, I dispelled some of their lies. I explained to her that they were correct that the court order for the baby to go home with us would be costly; however, it would not be her burden to carry, but ours. I hated for this adoption to go bad at the end of the pregnancy because of lies this agency uses to scare low income, pregnant women who are ignorant of the adoption details. It sickened me.

On the other hand, I wanted to be sure this birthmother did not have any doubts about giving her baby to us. I brought up the subject to her gently, explaining that I would absolutely love to raise her child and I would love the child with all my heart, but this baby is her baby, and if she wanted him to go to someone with no children who has been on a waiting list for years, it is her decision to make. I would understand. As I was saying this to her, she cut me off angrily, abruptly explaining to me, that she chose an adoptive family. She likes our family, she trusts our family, and she knows this would be our first baby and how much we had wanted a baby in our lives. With tears in my eyes, I advised her to simply not be there when the agency was to arrive at her house, putting a note on the door stating that she is not interested in their services or their incorrect information. This ended that issue, but another one arose.

It was now December, the month the baby was due, and the birthmother reinstated her prenatal doctor appointments. At one doctor appointment, she had a sonogram to see if the baby was healthy. She, of course, told them ahead of time that she wanted me involved as I was to be the adoptive mom. When the woman doing her sonogram asked the birthmother if she wanted to know if it was a boy or a girl, the birthmother looked at me, as if to ask me what I wanted. I stated that I did not want to know. The woman immediately blurted out to the birthmother that it was to be a baby boy. I sat there saddened that I could not experience the choice to know or the opportunity to be surprised.

At another doctor appointment, the birthmother asked the nurse to allow me to come into her appointment to hear the baby's heartbeat. The nurse snidely said that I could come in when called in. I waited at the edge of my seat. When I was called in, I rejoiced inside at the baby's heartbeat --- my baby's heartbeat. I had never experienced pregnancy and never cared to, but this made me understand the wonder and the miracle of a birth and made me realize that this baby would be mine someday. I wanted to listen to his heartbeat forever, but knew I had to leave the room eventually. I wanted to ask questions, but did not know what to ask. I floundered at the joy of it all, to ask a question. As I asked it, I knew it sounded a bit on the ignorant side, but I did not know the answer. The nurse answered the question as if I was a complete idiot and told me I had to leave the room now. I was heartbroken, but she could not completely crush me because I heard my baby's heart beating. I floated out of the room, with an air of sadness too, that a nurse could be so uncaring.

As the doctors were preparing for this baby's arrival, the personnel at the nearest hospital, declared that they do not do those kind of adoptions, and that she would have to find another hospital if she planned to give the baby up for private adoption. Our lawyer chided at the thought of that statement because it is the lawyer who does the adoption and legal documents, not the hospital, but there was nothing he could do if they were bent on making it difficult for us. This hospital was only a few short miles from her. The next local hospital would be a longer ride during winter months which scared me if she was going into labor, but we had no choice. She began to go to doctor appointments in that city to be closer to that hospital, and then it took much more time and gas to make the round-trips with her. It took me away from the other children for longer periods of time. James and I did not feel it was necessary to tell the other children in case it was another dead-end road. We wanted to spare them the disappointment and heartache. Excitedly though, this baby boy would be born in the same hospital as myself and three of my girls.

The Stork Arrives!

December came and went with nurses expressing excitement that the baby would be here any day. Weeks went by, then a month. I cannot describe the anticipation or the feeling that ran over me each time the phone rang, but my husband remained reserved. He was gearing himself up for yet another loss. Disappointment was no stranger to us, but good fortune had been. He knew if he was not flying high, the fall would not be so hard. He was also busy with law school and coaching our daughter's basketball team. I felt bad for James because he could not enjoy the anticipation of our first newborn baby, but I knew that he might be right. Nonetheless, we needed to be prepared with baby names. With James's law school schedule and exams, I was afraid our baby would be born and we would be unprepared. The baby's late arrival provided us the extra time we needed to discuss names. It was not easy, and I found myself getting frustrated with James. He did not care for the names I chose, and I did not care for the names he chose. When he came upon "Dawson," we both agreed and the frustration ended. We knew we had found the right name.

After a month of waiting, the birthmother's doctor decided to induce labor. The day came and I nervously picked her up at five o'clock in the morning for the big event. I knew this would be the tell-tale sign of whether or not she was going to allow James and me to adopt the baby. Surprisingly, she was already in labor and pacing the sidewalk when I picked her up at the scheduled time. I was so excited that she did not need to be induced. I was so nervous that I was numb. I was in the middle of an unfolding miracle and I had no idea what to say, how to sit, how to stand or what the birthmother expected from me. No one came to the hospital, not even the birth father. It was her and I. Even her doctor kept changing during the beginning of her labor.

It was my first birth, other than kittens and calves. I understood - a birth of any sort is a miracle. I was like a little child looking in amazement. I wish I could have encouraged the birth mom or been helpful. I stood awkwardly on the sidelines. I was filled with an overwhelming, nervous joy. There are not enough of words in the English language to describe such an amazing event. I was about to be a Mom of a newborn baby boy.

Unfortunately, we were not finished being treated poorly as birthmother and adoptive mother. I felt terrible for the birthmother. I wanted to protect her from the inconsiderate, hurtful doctors and nurses, but there was nothing I could do. I could not find the words. I did not feel like it was my place as the adoptive mother to speak up, but she was vulnerable and weakened by giving birth. The birthmother had made a point to say that she did not want to see the baby or hear him cry. The nurses and doctor intentionally kept the baby in the delivery room for what seemed like an eternity. At one point, while the baby was crying, the crowd of nurses split like the Red Sea for Moses — allowing the birthmother to have a clear view of the crying, needy newborn baby. My heart cried out for the newborn baby and the birthmother. I knew there was a close bond after enduring nine months of pregnancy, even though she had tried not to bond with him.

Several hours later, the birthmother was still in a hospital room. The doctor and nurses told her that she could not go home right away because her blood work revealed unsafe levels. We suspected that they were lying about the abnormal blood levels, but she did not dare leave without permission and potentially place the adoption at risk. She was treated like garbage by the hospital staff and sat in the hospital bed alone with no one checking on her.

She was finally allowed to leave an hour after her scheduled lawyer appointment. I drove her home, saddened that they delayed her to the point where she missed her appointment to sign the papers to finalize the adoption. I assumed a lawyer would never wait around for a no-show, but he was still in his office, so the birth parents signed the consent with no problem.

I was given a room in the hospital and stayed as the baby's mother. The nurses and doctors would not listen to me regarding any major decisions. The birthmother was called several times at home with questions about the baby. Each time exasperated, she would tell them that she had surrendered her parental rights and she had no right to make decisions.

Meanwhile, I was continually getting myself into trouble, inadvertently, of course. I told the nurses that this was my first baby and that I knew little about babies except for babysitting where every move is spelled out by the parent. Here I was, for the first time, holding my baby boy. I felt like I was assuming more responsibility than I could handle. I was overwhelmed with emotions. My mother could not come to the hospital because of a snowstorm. This kept other potential visitors away. Despite the weather, James had to coach Brittani's basketball game, but he came with all the kids after practice. I felt alone and ignorant but, on the other hand, I was ready for the challenge and content holding him. I stared at his every move.

I felt like it was too good to be true. I wondered, I prayed, I was scared, I was excited, I was content. No one had told me to feed him. I thought the nurses would have fed him, but I do not know if they ever did. I am not sure to this day if they ever fed him. He was born in the morning and I did not feed him until 3 pm when I realized a small bottle was sitting on his hospital crib. I asked about this bottle and was condescendingly told that I could feed him. How would I know? The only time I had fed a baby this young, I had it warmed up and was told it was feeding time. I had begged for direction from the nurses on staff and explained my newness to motherhood several times.

Dawson was so content and sweet, he never screamed to eat. However, I have read since then that an adopted baby misses his mother's scent, voice and touch. Therefore, they can be in shock and quiet.

Before he saw the doctor, a nurse cleaned my baby boy up, wrapped him tightly in his blanket and gave him to me to talk to and hold. I was feeling motherly and unwrapped him, talked to him and stared at his cute little baby body. Then a nurse walked in, and angrily scolded me for unwrapping him because he was all ready for the doctor. She spent the next three seconds re-wrapping him and then stormed out of the room. I smirked to myself. She was right. I wasted a whole three seconds of her day with my stupidity and desire to look at my newborn son.

After his birth, his birthmother told me the rest of the story (as Paul Harvey would say). The birthmother had seriously considered me for adopting a child of hers before Dawson was born, but had changed her mind. One day, after we had met, she passed me in the hallway of the doctor's office when I was talking to my youngest son, Samuel. I was trying to encourage him to be compliant with his blood test to check for any diseases or problems. Because he was from a third world country, it was extremely important for him to have blood work done. I explained to him in his native language that they were going to "jook" him, and I gently pinched his arm to show him how the needle would feel. The birthmother and father pushed a baby stroller by me at that moment and were impressed by my compassion and love for this little three-year-old in my lap. In the back of her mind, she says, she always knew she was going to carry my baby. She did not know if she was going to do a surrogate situation or what, but she felt that someday she was to carry my baby.

Months after seeing me at the doctor's office, she found out she was pregnant. She was sitting in the abortion clinic to abort Dawson. She did not believe in abortion, but knew that she had too much on her plate and could not raise another child at this point in her life. She had two children with special needs and she knew this unborn baby would never get the attention he would need. As she was sitting in the waiting room, my face and my desire to adopt a baby bombarded her thoughts. Minutes before her name was called to abort her unborn baby, she left the abortion clinic. She walked home. At that moment, she knew that I was the one to raise her baby boy. She immediately called our mutual friend, whom I had met as a result of my letter to the editor several years before. She told this mutual friend to contact me and ask me to adopt her baby when she gave birth.

I remember that phone call clearly. I remember the excitement, but was reserved because birth parents in our state can change their mind up until 45 days after they surrender their rights. There were many days in between. To make this story more unbelievable, I remember clearly that moment with my son Samuel, explaining to him why he needed his blood drawn, and thinking at the same time that I wished someone would see me. I wished someone would see who I am and how I am with my children instead of believing my hurting girls' lies. I wished that someone who was pregnant with a baby and did not want to keep it, would see me with my children and see that I was caring and decide to give me their baby. As the birthmother told her side of the story, my jaw dropped, knowing that it was the mirror image of my story.

Our Life & A Baby

Our older girls, Brittani and Chloe, always said that they wished that we would adopt a baby girl. My rebuttal was always that I did not exactly turn down a baby girl. I agreed with them that it would be fun to have a baby in the house to lighten things up a bit. If I had a choice, I preferred to have a baby boy because I was better with boys than girls. I do not enjoy the emotional nature of girls. I would not be able to turn down a child in need based on their gender. I put it in God's hands.

When Dawson was born, we had seven children in the home. Oldest to youngest, we had Jadin, Brittani, Chloe, Toni, Josh, Samuel and Dawson. Everyone loved Dawson, Josh and Samuel. I was hoping that these young ones would pull our family together, and for the most part they did that for a time. However, Brittani, Chloe and Toni, set out to destroy our family. I do not know if they did it consciously, at least not at first, but their trauma controlled them and their trauma wreaked havoc.

Even though Brittani and Chloe were excited to have a newborn in our family, Brittani immediately had an attitude when she visited Dawson at the hospital. She could not express any joy. She disliked the name we chose for our baby. James and I had been trying to adopt a baby for five years and were thrilled that we were now in a hospital room with our first baby. We ignored Brittani's continuous negativity. Brittani was upset because she could not hold the new baby first. She assumed that she would be the first one, but she had a virus and we worried about exposing Dawson. Instead of being understanding, she was miserable and wanted everyone else miserable – when we were not she became more miserable. Our homestudy social worker felt that having a baby in the house would show the older children how a baby should be treated. They would see a child have a healthy childhood and gain an understanding of why they were taken away from their birth parents.

At home, life was the same. Brittani's mood dictated the family's mood. I tried to set the mood, but Brittani's antics trumped my efforts. She was absolutely miserable all of the time and wanted everyone to know it. She wanted everyone around her to be miserable. If I refused to be miserable and continued to float around the house happily, she would toss her head to the side quickly in disgust as I walked by. Eventually, after a tiring day of this treatment, I would break down and become miserable and short with the children. Only then would Brittani smile.

When Brittani was good, she was terrific. She helped with the baby a great deal since James was in law school and I was working nights. I loved my job and I loved my clients. They called me the "energizer bunny" as they watched me scoot around the house, preparing it and cleaning it for the next day. I would restock bathrooms, clean messes and get on my hands and knees to scrub the filthy parts of the floor, all while being as quiet as I could to allow them to sleep. My favorite thing to do was to make the beautiful woodwork shine. I cared about the details. I took my job seriously and was grateful to have the job.

Amazingly, I could only get four days off for Dawson's birth. It broke my heart to go back to work when he was four days old. I wanted to quit my job, but we needed the benefits. If I had given birth, I would have been given more time. On my work nights if he woke in the night Brittani was on duty. James could not get up in the night because he was in law school and he could not afford to be exhausted. We all agreed on this plan.

Dawson would wake in the night crying for his bottle or to be cuddled with and put back into his crib. After snuggling back into bed, warming my cold body in the cold sheets, occasionally Samuel would scream loudly. I would rush to his side to comfort him and to prevent him from waking Dawson back up. I would take Samuel and Josh to the bathroom and hold Samuel until he calmed. Sometimes, I would lie next to him in his bed, to let him know I was there for him. In hindsight, James and I have concluded that Josh would wake Samuel up abruptly, causing him to scream in terror, rather than him getting a parent to help him go to the bathroom. At age fourteen, Josh still has difficulty understanding that a parent's role is to help him and allow him to be a child. Josh has stretches where he urinates out his window and in his closet for no apparent reason – we have not figured it out.

On nights I had to work, Brittani was responsible for waking up if the boys needed someone in the night. Most of the time, they did not. James was responsible for getting good grades in law school, which he was able to do despite the stress at home. Interestingly, getting up to give Dawson a bottle at night would incapacitate Brittani the next day. She would spend most of her day upstairs in her room sleeping and relaxing. On snowy winter days, I would go directly to Brittani's shoveling job because I did not want to go back out in bad weather. I would shovel for hours so that Brittani could remain inside where she enjoyed it the most, watching Dawson. I would get home hours after my nightshift ended, handing Brittani the shoveling money. I was not able to pay Brittani for watching Dawson, but I paid her the shoveling money.

My mother noticed how much Brittani did for us, so she bought her an expensive camera for her birthday. I never wanted my children to feel like they were being used and not appreciated or compensated. So, it made me feel good that she was getting these extra surprises. Her babysitting shift was normally only a half-hour shift in the night and an hour in the morning.

It went well for the most part, but I found that because of Brittani's unpredictable and irritable attitude, I could not ask her to watch the children during the day so I could take a nap, so the only sleep I got was the broken sleep at work. I crashed during my three days off. I became extremely irritable, but tried hard to sustain. After my third trip to the emergency room in two years, James made me quit. He said we would figure out the health insurance and live off of the student loans. I felt terrible. I felt like I had failed him. He insisted to the point that I had to submit. He was right. The third trip to the emergency room made it obvious that the lack of sleep and the stress at home caused by Brittani, was slowly killing me from the inside out. I had good intentions to take a nap at least once a week, but it could not happen consistently. She acted as if giving the baby one bottle during the night was an insurmountable

145

burden. We bought into the Cobra plan at my work to cover our family's insurance needs.

Six months after Dawson's birth, on the same day I finished my master's degree in Practical Theology, we finalized and celebrated our first baby's adoption day. Dawson was now ours legally. We were not the only ones relieved. Dawson's birth mother was sighing with relief also. She knew this adoption was what was best for Dawson and could relax now that it was finalized. I think she was afraid that her emotions would screw things up for us.

A year after Dawson was born, we changed churches looking for a closer relationship with the Lord. I wanted to hear and learn more of what the Bible has for us and I did not feel fulfilled where we were. (I Chronicles 22:19) I was hungry for the Word of God and felt starved. I loved a handful of people at the church we were going to, but most of them did not know who we were or cared to say hello. The church was in a white community known for not accepting anyone, except wealthy white people. It was time for our multi-ethnic family to move on. We decided to land at a church where we knew the pastor and his wife from basketball and soccer games at a nearby Christian School. Our children had played sports with their son.

The new church was alive, welcoming, and had a good wholesome message. It challenged us. The sermons spoke to our lives. I was ready to grow spiritually, and James and I prayed our children would grow spiritually. We felt loved at the new church. We belonged. The people who attended the church seemed genuine and compassionate. The children's church was alive and actively pursuing a relationship with Jesus. Over the next few years, we became heavily involved in the church. I was only asked to help with nursery, which I did not enjoy because most of the babies belonged to first-time mothers who sat in the nursery with the baby anyway. I hated missing church to sit with parents and their children and do nothing. James was more involved. He was asked to be the church board secretary because he was an attorney. He was also asked to teach an adult Sunday school class for a five-week session.

James and I believed in being active in church. We attended every event. If the church doors were open, we were there. Church was important to us and was a priority. I had a good foundation coming from the Methodist Church in a small town, and James had enjoyed that church when we were first married and had our first three children. To this day, I am grateful for that foundation.

When Brittani, Chloe and Toni began to have adoptive issues (post-traumatic stress symptoms), we allowed them to go to youth group and participate in all of the special activities the new church offered. We never withheld church activities no matter how bad their behaviors were. We encouraged them to go to God during times of need.

Unfortunately, they were not going to God, but were targeting people in our new church to serve as their allies. Chloe spent hours dramatically crying to the youth group leader's wife about imagined hardships at home. Brittani attended Sunday church worship with a sour expression. She stood in the back of the church during worship and made sure everyone noticed that she refused to sit with us. Toni would sit with us, but would flop her body down in her chair and looked as if she was behind bars. We thought these outward displays of disrespect were normal for teenagers and that others in the congregation would know that they had broken hearts from their youth.

We were wrong. The girls were circulating untrue rumors to the church leaders and their families. Brittani's unwarranted behavior in church served to add credence to the rumors and highlighted our poor parenting and dysfunctional home. James and I have learned that very few people understand adoptive children, but we were particularly disappointed by the fact that no one sat us down and talked to us about it. No one asked if there was anything they could do to help our family. None of the adult "leaders" approached us about the awful things our daughters were saying about us. For the most part, we remained clueless about the extent of our girls' slander. We mistakenly thought the people in this church understood. Our reputations and character were dragged through the muck and mire behind our backs. We went to church thinking everything was fine, but we began to see subtle changes and hear familiar subtle words spoken over us. What these same people did not realize, is that we were told enough information that would have jeopardized their custody of their children, their place in the church and their jobs, but we knew our girls' tendency to exaggerate and fabricate.

Prayers on our behalf became slanted to what they were hearing from our girls instead of our cries for help, or God's Word for our lives. Church members believed the girls' disrespect and meanness was justified by our alleged terrible parenting.

I wondered why I was never asked to be on any type of prayer committee or teach Sunday school even though I was ordained through the seminary I had taken classes through. I wondered why when the orphanage director came to visit us from oversees she was not allowed to speak in church for five minutes, speak at a church luncheon, or at youth group. Only one person in the congregation came over to her to greet her, though all of the leaders knew she was there. I wondered why no one in the church sought to get to know us, when we frequently invited people over. We took several couples in the church out to dinner in an attempt to form closer relationships with them, but nothing ever materialized. I wondered why every conversation I had with the pastor's wife and her older married daughters, left me confused and feeling like a second-class citizen. I wondered why I could not get the pastor's wife to pray over my daughters when I frequently told her about our troubles with them. The girls' anger and craziness got ridiculous and I begged for help to no avail.

The pastor's wife claimed to understand abuse and PTSD from her own past, but she never helped. Instead, she allied herself with our traumatized girls without attempting to get to the root of their problems. For a long time, we had no idea where the criticism and judgmental comments were coming from, but over time, we caught on and the many talks we had with our girls, we recognized more and more the twisted perceptions of us and the things around them. Any mistakes that we made were compounded in their damaged brains, and any consequences or punishments were seen as nothing more than our meanness and cruelty. Any good that we did was not trusted. Rather it was viewed as an ulterior motive, and therefore twisted into something bad.

Our girls were looking for an audience for their drama and the pastor's wife fit the bill. She would end a talk with me with, "If your daughter comes to me, I will pray over her." It did not matter to her that these girls were tormenting us at home. It broke my heart. I wanted so badly for my children to understand God's transformational power and love. I wanted them to feel His presence and know that He was God. I wanted them to heal from their horrendous past that was destroying their present. I did not want to lose them too. We had already lost Jesslyn and Miguel. My heart had already been crushed. We continued to pray heartfelt prayers aloud, in their rooms at night, as well as silent prayers as a couple and by ourselves. We badly wanted to see a change in them, for their sake, more than ours. We had hopes for their future.

A few years after we began attending this new church, the Pastor's son died in a tragic car accident. He was recklessly driving at high speed and hit a tree on the side of a road. No one expected him to die. Everyone expected a miracle. He was expected to take over as pastor when his father retired. Their son was anointed. When he used to lead worship, we could feel the Lord's presence. It was amazing. He sang from the depths of his heart and opened our hearts. His death, was a crushing blow to his family, his steady girlfriend and the congregation. The church never recovered. The sermons no longer spoke to us, but left us confused.

The main theme became, "If you do not get on board with us, you are going to miss the boat." In other words, if you do not agree with how we worship and pray, you are going to be left behind and miss out on experiencing God's presence. I had never heard this before. The Bible says that God meets us where we are at and is waiting for us to accept Him. (Luke 19:10) God is available day and night and loves us dearly. We do not have to work our way to God. God has worked His way to us. He sent His only son to suffer a horrific death on a cross, taking on everyone else's sins, to give us eternal life. (John 3:16) Believing in Christ should lead to freedom.

The Bible does not say we are going to miss out on God if we do not conform. (Romans 5:8) We may miss out on some blessings if we do not press in, but He wants all of His children to join Him in heaven. (John 3:16) He is asking for us all to come, but knows that some will reject Him, and He understands that we are all in a different part of our journey with Him.

A Troubled Child

Before James traveled overseas to retrieve our young boys, we took in a little girl for a short time in order for her family to be rejuvenated and prepared to better handle her behaviors. Rebekka was a seven-year old girl with a thin stature and short boyish hair. She came to our home as a troubled child that was not doing well in her adoptive home. Her adoptive home was struggling a great deal with her behaviors and finding themselves resorting to unethical ways of dealing with her.

We took her in for a few weeks, and we all immediately fell in love with her. Knowing how adoptive children often have what is known as a honeymoon period, I did not assume she was an angel and the adoptive parents were the problem. However, we all felt a special connection with her. Brittani, especially loved Rebekka. Rebekka was special to her. I think Brittani saw herself in Rebekka. When Rebekka went home, we were all heartbroken, but we knew that we were only keeping her for a short time.

A few months later, we took Rebekka again. Not surprisingly, she did very well. We were extra firm and a bit short with her. We wanted to test the waters - to see how she would respond. We wanted to make sure that respite at our house was not like going to summer camp. I did not want her to like it more with us because that is not the point of respite. We made a point to be strict with her. Each time I gave her a chore or spoke firmly to her, she responded respectfully, timely and happily. I could not exactly punish that.

And so it went. Rebekka came and went two more times before her adoptive father decided that their family could not handle her behavioral issues. They were also struggling with Anna, the younger, non-related girl they adopted from the same orphanage at the same time as Rebekka. They were hopeful that Anna's behavior would improve without Rebekka.

I knew that the behaviors Rebekka displayed in her first adoptive home would not disappear. I hoped that when her behaviors resurfaced, we would have a strong enough bond with her to work through anything. Unfortunately, one thing James and I have learned in this adoptive journey, is that many adoptive children intentionally sabotage and destroy their relationships. They willingly cut family ties and destroy their future in a flash without looking back. Adoptive children are accustomed to being thrown away, and many times they will inadvertently throw away everything they ever had during an emotional crisis. Unfortunately, Rebekka was no different.

In the beginning, Rebekka was respectful, helpful and loveable. She fit our family like a glove. She belonged. A few weeks after arriving, she called me "Mom." After Rebekka called me mom, James overheard Josh lashing out at her in disgust, "You called her Mom!"

Rebekka replied, "I called her Mom because I love her."

I was happy that she was feeling loved and felt safe enough to reciprocate that love. From that day forward, she called me Mom. For each child, it has been a bit different. For our first two boys, their innate disrespect made it necessary for us to refer to ourselves as Mom and Dad and insist that they do from day one. For Kyle, who was sixteen years old and over six feet tall when he came, we never pushed it. It was awkward for him to call us mom and dad, but he found a happy medium. He did not want to show disrespect by calling us by our first names. However, he did not typically use Mom or Dad. When addressing me, he would walk in the room, clear his throat and say, "Ummm." That was my cue to look up. However, for most of our children, we insisted they call us Mom and Dad from the beginning as a sign of respect and authority.

I frequently caught Brittani and Chloe being rude to Rebekka. I was amazed at how mean they were. Rebekka was kind to everyone. When it was time for Rebekka to go home from respite, Brittani would cry for her to stay. I expected her to be welcomed with open arms when she was adopted, but I should have known better. Brittani and Chloe had been bitter and jealous when we adopted their younger sister Toni - unfortunately, Rebekka was an unsuspecting target.

Closure for Rebekka

Rebekka received the same considerations all of our children did with respect to staying in contact with her former family. We know that when we adopt, we are adopting our children's past and current hurts and traumas. We have learned that love alone does not fix adoptive children. We have always tried to give them closure by bringing together their past lives with their present lives, closing the gaps and mending fresh wounds. While necessary, we understand that our attempts to provide closure were not a cure-all. We also believe in providing closure for their former family or families regardless of the reasons they were unable to raise the children.

We drove our family five hours north to visit Rebekka's first adoptive home. She had lived there for two years (interrupted by numerous respite stays) after being adopted from an orphanage in her home country in Africa.

We had a good time getting to know them, but it was obvious how some of their ways were not consistent with an African child's mindset and expectations. For example, this family did not understand how valued food was to their African children. Our African children were malnourished and have been hungrier than any American can comprehend. This family did not plan meals at any particular intervals. When insecurities revolving around food increases, adoptive children (especially those from orphanages) revert to taking care of themselves by stealing and hoarding food. We have learned the importance of adoptive families providing three meals a day at regular times each day. Despite taking care of their needs, several of our children continued to steal and hoard. In many cases, they preferred to steal food. Leaving it out on the counter, announcing that it could be eaten at any time, did not guarantee we would see it be eaten. It will disappear quickly and silently. I have heard this behavior referred to as 'feral cat behavior.'

There were several biological children in Rebekka's former adoptive family, some older and out of the home, and some still in the home. They also had two other adopted children, Anna and Shane. When we visited, Anna was struggling just as Rebekka had struggled in their home. Anna was struggling greatly with adoptive issues, inappropriate orphanage behaviors and bonding. Anna's adoptive mother was exacerbated, completely overwhelmed by Anna's behavior. After our visit, I decided there was no way I would take Anna on respite if they asked. She was too much for our family to handle. She was an awkward, homely little child, who lacked social skills and a knowledge of appropriate behavior. I felt awful for these parents who had a heart for adoption, but did not seem to enjoy this third-world transplant.

College Bound

The walls that came tumbling down and were rebuilt many times with our teenagers, stayed standing for quite a while. Brittani went off to college about three hours away. With her rejection and insecurity issues stemming from her childhood, she acted like she was being pushed out of the house and rejected. To show her that college is a natural, positive transition, we bought her a cell phone to give her the feeling that she could call home anytime. We also bought her a car so she would feel like she could come home anytime. During her first year, I mailed her cookies, her bathing suit, letters from home, special final exam packages, and anything else she requested. We visited her several times her first two years, attending parents' weekend and joining her in the dining hall for dinner on several other occasions. We wanted her to know that we were not far away and that she was still part of our family. She loved showing us around her campus, introducing us to her friends, and having her younger siblings spend the night during parents' weekend. She also brought home some friends to stay at our house on a couple of weekends. Our relationship with Brittani has never been stronger than it was during her first two years of college. We thought she had conquered her insecurities.

During a winter break, we all traveled several states away to visit colleges for Chloe. She wanted to live out of state, which I thought was adventurous. James and I supported her plan. I brought Dawson, who was now one-year-old. He had a cold or flu during the trip. He had a fever every night that we battled with medication, a nebulizer and cool baths, while during the day he seemed fine. His illness made the three thousand miles of driving in six days seem more insane than it already was. I felt bad for the little guy. I did everything I could to break the fever.

While traveling, I paid for the girls' big brother to take a train to meet us. We had not seen him since he had moved out of state. He spent a day with us. I then brought him to visit his birth father who lived nearby. I was not sure how his birth father would view me, but he immediately gave me a huge hug and cried like a baby on my shoulder. He thanked me many times for what James and I had done for his son and for the three girls. That meant so much to me. So many times, adoptive parents are viewed as the enemy (as thieves), but he welcomed me with open arms.

Chloe decided to attend college a few states away from us, but we supported her decision like we had done with Brittani.

Chloe wanted to try out for cheerleading. Both James and I knew that she would not make the team because she was not that talented or passionate about cheerleading. In high school, she was a cheerleader for a year but spent no extra time getting in shape or being flexible enough to do the special moves. We wanted to encourage her to branch out, so we arranged for her to attend cheerleading tryouts in the middle of the summer before she enrolled for her freshman year. She did not make the team, but seemed to appreciate that we had sacrificed for her.

While attending this college, we attended parents' weekends to reassure her that while she was away at college, she had not left our family. We also sent cookies in the mail and special college bed sheets and letters from the family. Chloe left with my high school ring on her finger. I reluctantly gave it to her, as I wore it all the time and loved it, but I wanted her to have a part of me so that she knew I was always with her and proud of her. I knew how much she needed a Mom and needed to feel loved. To this day, she still has the ring despite not speaking for nearly four years. We expect that Chloe will reach out to us in an effort to reconnect – although we are not holding our breath.

Another Girl, Are You Kidding Me?

Before we adopted Rebekka, I had said I did not want to adopt any more girls. It is fun to listen to different perspectives on raising girls versus raising boys and who enjoys which gender the most. James and I are straightforward people, and our girls were always too emotional, played head games and seemed ready to destroy their futures at a moment's notice. Our girls were much more jealous than our boys and had difficulties getting along, even though we had a large house with plenty of space to get away from each other and had plenty to do.

We had our troubles with the boys, but I had made a point to say, "No more girls." God likes to stretch us. Not that He goes out of His way to give us what we do not want, but He does things His way in His time for His glory and apparently, He wanted me to have more girls. Rebekka was the first girl to arrive after my ban on girls and Anna was the second - the girl I had made a point to say that I would not help out with, let alone adopt.

At the end of James's last semester of law school, I had been exchanging emails with Rebekka's former adoptive family. I had tried to guide them through difficult times with Anna and Rebekka. I was not an expert, but my personal library consisted of an array of books about behavior modification, adoption, effects of foster care, fetal alcohol syndrome, surviving abuse, and other related topics. We had vast experience. I was confident that I had adoptive tips to share, and plenty of compassion and understanding; and sometimes adoptive parents do not need other people's advice or opinions as much as they need to be heard and understood. I can serve that role because I have been through an array of scenarios and because of that, have become less judgmental.

It came to a point when I felt a wave of compassion for this mother who was desperate and drowning in her frustrations and anger toward Anna. I knew it was no longer good for Anna, as with Rebekka, to be in that home, nor was it good for that mother to be with Anna. Her approaches did not work, and the stress was rising like an out-of-control bonfire. I asked James if I could offer to take Anna in while her adoptive family searched for a new home for her. As with Rebekka, Anna was likely headed to an out-of-state group home. James was extremely busy studying for the bar exam, so he agreed we could take her only if I felt that I was up for the challenge by myself. I said I was and within a few days, we had Anna on respite.

When most people are given some peace and space, they feel like they can handle the situation better, so Anna went home after about a month of being with us. It did not work, and she landed on our doorstep once again. This time we offered to adopt her. She seemed to be a different person at our house. I did not see the behaviors that the adoptive family experienced. Again, I caution all adoptive parents to be careful with this line of thinking as there is what is typically known as a honeymoon period. However, I felt that the adoptive mother was looking at the behaviors and was missing something. Anna's so-called manipulation seemed to be a cognitive disorder. Later, this was confirmed by an expert neuropsychologist we had retained who taught us how to tailor her studies and life to her learning style.

We never disregarded what another adoptive parent said, even if we saw things differently. For example, the previous adoptive parent saw a great deal of inappropriate sexual behaviors and said that Anna would get up in the night. We listened and put a door alarm on her door at night so that we could hear her if she got up at night. She never did. We also do not let her alone with our boys at any time in a different part of the house or where there is no supervision. We take precautions even if we do not see the behavior. We have seen glimpses of inappropriate behaviors and reinstituted strict boundaries where necessary. Overall, she is a good girl and wants to please, but her cognitive delays disrupt her judgment and appropriateness at times. She struggles with stress and is susceptible to orphanage behaviors. It is something we will always have to be conscious of.

James left for another part of the state to take the bar exam and passed it with flying colors. Given the stress and chaos caused by Brittani, Chloe and Toni and the additions of five children to our family, that was nothing short of a miracle.

Our lawyer told James it is not wise to make any major changes during law school. Interestingly, James picked up Josh and Samuel in Africa when he was preparing for law school. James studied a great deal for the LSAT because he wanted to get a good scholarship, which he did. During his second year of law school, we welcomed our first newborn baby into our home, then Rebekka and lastly, Anna. While it is true that it is not wise to make any major changes during law school, when God is leading you, He can do amazing things in your life and through your obedience.

Violent Fits of Rage

I saw a glimpse of the war our African children endured. I saw how the war broke out in their country. The war between neighbors, between tribes, and between people that once had no problem with each other. I saw first-hand what happens to people under extreme stress. I spent a year refereeing episodic violence-filled fits of rage, and I was scared. I thought I could prevent the rage by talking, recognizing the warning signs, or not provoking them to anger. None of my tactics worked. These kids were like lions lying in wait for their prey. Seemingly out of nowhere, they would begin by staring. At this point, it was too late. There was nothing I could do to redirect, bypass or talk them down. It was time for battle.

The smallest things angered them. For example, Rebekka had begun to open the teacher's manual for math and I scolded her quietly for touching it; Samuel did not want to get into the car to go pick up Toni at piano lessons because he was busy playing in the sand pile; and Josh was told he could have snack if he washed his hands first. Something triggered a reaction in their brains that could not be defused. Nothing deterred them from having a fit – even when their friends or our family came over or called.

If I responded with anger, their violent fit worsened and quickly became unmanageable. If I responded passively, they lashed out to injure and inflict damage. During their fits, they had no regard for anyone's safety or well-being. Samuel was remorseful afterwards, and we were able to use this to help him break the cycle. I tried to talk them down while restraining them the best I could. I talked and I prayed. I loved and I was careful. I mostly dodged blows and kicks. It was so sad to watch these beautiful children turn into such savage beasts. They could not hear me as I spoke. Samuel was a mama's boy, so I kept repeating, "Samuel, it is me. Samuel, it is me, Mama." But he could not hear me, and his eyes were glazed over so that he could not see. After his violent fits, which usually lasted an hour or more, Samuel would hold me so tightly, I thought I would break. He would hold me and cry from the inner depths of his heart. He could not stop. I would say, "It is OK," over and over again. He was so sorry. He was scared of his own emotions and actions. I could feel his deep remorse, but initially it did not stop him from repeating the cycle.

This went on with each child almost daily for a year. I am not sure what triggered it, but it was a horrifying experience for our family. A friend stopped by during a fit and was shocked and left speechless. She has never forgotten the look on the child's face and the violence and screaming. We thought it was spiritual but the church leaders would not help us.

We had hired a carpenter from our church to do repairs and electrical work. Thinking back, I wonder if it was some type of spiritual oppression. Despite our church's understanding of spiritual bondage and deliverance, this carpenter never offered to talk to my child, hold them down for me, pray over them or pray for me. There were times when he watched me get punched and trying to dodge the next blow. He acted like it was normal for me to have to hold my child down while he screamed bloody murder. He thought I was paying the price for provoking my son. He was the carpenter coming in to do his business. He did not ask and he was not going to help. I always thought that this was odd. His first day on the job, he prayed in the kitchen with James and I. When I tried to explain what all the screaming was about, I was met with a blank uncaring look. Later, I discovered that Toni was spreading the same rumors that we were terrible parents as Brittani and Chloe had for years. Looking back, Toni's rumors, combined with seeing me try to deal with these uncontrollable violent fits of rage every day, made our home look like complete chaos and anger and violence. Taken out of context, the fits supported the girls' rumors.

The same carpenter from church was asked to check out our television set, as it had stopped working abruptly. He found a penny burned between the television plug and the outlet. This nearly burned our house down. It was slowly smoldering and should have caught on fire in the night, but it did not. Once again, we had been saved from destruction and potential tragedy. After questioning the children, we concluded Josh was the culprit. We had become highly skilled at reading their facial expressions, eye contact, eye movement and voice inflection to detect the egregious liars. We were right. He finally confessed and told us he did it when he was pretending to clean the living room while I was in the next room painting. He had told me he had to go to the bathroom and while there, he got an assortment of items to experiment sticking in the socket. When he did not get any reaction from sticking these items into the socket, he tried a penny. He was scared by the sparks and walked away.

While we were dealing with daily fits, Josh began urinating on his bedroom floor, between his mattresses, and in his hollow bedpost nightly. After destroying a third mattress set, we had Josh sleep on the floor with several blankets acting as a buffer from the floor. We begged him to stop urinating in his room and we showed him the damage he was doing to the ceiling below. It made no difference. He kept urinating on his carpet, and the odor was incredibly disgusting.

I understand that this behavior was stemming from unaddressed past emotional trauma and confusion, but regardless of the reason, urinating on the floor was wrong. Despite our desire to end it quickly, he continued to piss in his room for 2-1/2 years. At one point, we gave him a choice: we could send his parents' village money or spend $1,800.00 on a floor. He chose to continue to urinate and we had to buy a new floor rather than send his parents' village money. His urine penetrated the vinyl flooring we had put in. A gluten free diet helped, but we do not know if it addressed the root cause.

It has always been something with Josh. His behaviors are constant and draining. He had the warmest room in the house, but he kept putting his thermostat up to extremely high temperatures, which resulted in an inflated electricity bill and dangerously hot heating vents. He also liked putting paper in the heater coil "to see what would happen." When we put a locked case over the top of the thermostat, he jammed a variety of small pieces of carpet, pins and nails in the keyhole and edges, until we could no longer unlock it to turn on the heat each night. We also noticed that the top of his baseboard heater was caving in. He was standing on it to look into the bathroom window. I am scared to think who may have been changing while he was peering in on them. He carved the number 13 into his cherry closet door. Jesus had been carved into our kitchen table and numerous carvings have been found on the front porch chairs. Like Drake, he cannot be unsupervised for a moment - he is a ninja.

Parenting

Parents normally do the best they can. A good friend of mine, who has since passed away, always told me if parents do the best they can with what they have and know – at that moment in time- they did well. I have to admit; we were terribly naïve when we first adopted. I thought that any child, given enough support, love, structure and outlets for their anger and pain, would change and grow to be a productive member of society. We have learned that you cannot force a child to change, no matter how hard you try or how hard you try to deter them and sometimes they do not want to change. They will ultimately choose who they want to be.

We were not perfect, but we were perfect for each of our children. I believe we were what our children needed in their lives. We loved them dearly, gave them everything we had in us, and supported them in every good and righteous endeavor. We provided love and understanding no matter how we were treated in return. We were the only ones who were willing to point out when they were wrong and try to correct their illogical and unrealistic thinking. I certainly faltered many times by becoming angry and saying things I should not have said. Regardless, we loved them through their difficulties. Many times we tried too hard. We mistakenly spoiled them when we should have been hard on them.

Of all of the gifts we felt we could give our children, the greatest was stability. James and I emulated a strong, healthy marriage and did not waiver in our commitment to one another. We also showed our children that we were committed to them. Our children were adopted and did not bounce from home to home ever again. They were brought up in one home and they were loved. The danger Drake brought to our lives was a different story, and we knew he needed extensive supervision, therapy and a residential setting. For Jesslyn, on the other hand, we were only reaching out for a psychological evaluation, not for long-term housing. All of our children were good at displaying behaviors and attitudes that would have easily gotten them moved from any other foster or adoptive home, but James and I hung on tight and refused to budge.

James and I stayed in close contact and we knew when we were floundering. We sought help when we felt we needed it or one of our children needed it, but we consistently struggled to find the right kind of help. Everyone can give up on my child – therapists, teachers, school superintendents, schools, coaches, and group leaders --- but I cannot. They are our children. I legally cannot and emotionally will not give up on my children. On the other hand, I have had to readjust my expectations for some children. For Drake and Jesslyn, I sought help from psychiatric evaluations, group homes, and rehabs, but we were deemed the bad guys. The root causes from the severe abuse and neglect were ignored and tucked under a rug, so that we could become the focus. No one made them accountable for their behaviors or actions, but instead continued to point their fingers at us. We were deemed to be the bad guys in Drake's situation, but then the residential treatment facility was forced to employ more staff because of his violence and non-compliant behaviors. If they could not handle him, why were we expected to? We were deemed the bad guys in the case of Jesslyn, but the psychiatric hospital/residential facility put her in a padded room and gave her a dose of an antipsychotic before shipping her off to another residential treatment facility because her behaviors were too much for them. I do not have a padded room, and I can assure you if I put one of my angry children in a padded room that they could not get out of, it would be deemed as abuse. If they could not handle her, then why was I expected to? I do not have a stash of PRN (as needed) anti-psychotic drugs, nor would it be appropriate for me to use it in that way. So, why are we the bad guys? Why are we being judged under a microscope? If they could not handle her behaviors without a padded room and anti-psychotic drugs, then why was I expected to? One church member was judgmental and critical of us, and she admittedly had taken in her foster sister years ago for her mother who was struggling with her behaviors. At the first sign of difficulty, she got rid of her and shipped her back to her mother. How did she feel she had the right to criticize and judge us? We have been wholly committed to our children and have, if anything, given them too much credit and too many chances.

We also noticed that our children could not wait for help when they started to deteriorate into crisis mode. It often took weeks or months to get needed mental health appointments, and even then, the therapist or psychiatrist needed several appointments to get to know their new client. Meanwhile, our home would become a war zone and there were numerous occasions when we had to call the police and engage crisis mental health services – including in-patient psychiatric stays for four of our children. We were also well-read on topics relating to our children's backgrounds, current needs and diagnoses. A consistent pattern arose. I noticed that the professionals did not read the same books or ascribe to the same theories. For example, each book I read would emphasize the adoptive parents' role in therapy and the need for family therapy, and yet, when I suggested these options, I was ignored and ridiculed. When I strongly advocated for Rebekka during one of her meltdowns, the hospital's social worker called child protective services, reporting me for not understanding my daughter's diagnosis and for blaming my child for her problems. I was merely trying to educate the social worker about the overarching impact of trauma. When Drake and Jesslyn entered in-patient treatment facilities, we were never part of their therapy. So their treatment providers only heard a one-sided view of what happened. The perceptions of a hurting, angry child can be slanted and are often not based in reality. It was obvious that they were not working with these children to go home or to re-build a relationship with us.

Brittani, Chloe and Toni did not warrant psychiatric facilities, but bullied and intimidated me. I constantly tried to appease them. Everything I did or said, was second guessed by them. I became a second class citizen in my home. We became prisoners of our own home. Their ammunition was enough to keep us at bay and obedient to them. They learned how to balance their nastiness with manipulation and fake caring. They would talk sweetly to me in order to get what they wanted. I became too soft and I believe we have paid for spoiling them. Regardless, I doubt being harder on them would have prevented their twisted thinking, belief system, and distorted reality.

I began to experience the effects of some undiagnosed health problems under the stress of raising these three girls. My medical problems interfered with my parenting and created more fear. I was afraid of who they were becoming and of what was happening to me. I had a short temper and higher expectations that they could not meet. I was impatient and frustrated, which quickly turned to anger and bitterness. It was not healthy for me. I suffered from dizziness, confusion, agitation, irritability and weakness at random times. I frequently overate and gained much unneeded weight, because I was looking for energy and comfort from food. I often woke up in the night with heart-attack-type symptoms, pain in my arm, and my heart beating rapidly. I began to lose my voice, which all my doubters attributed to my yelling at the children too much. The more I tried to say that it was not the problem, the more people made assumptions and smiled awkwardly at me. I tried many different self-remedies as well as explain my symptoms to every doctor I had, including the emergency room doctors.

I regularly explained to my kids that I did not feel right, and to stay out of my way and not be unruly or pick at each other. I knew at these times that I could not handle it. I did not feel right. My head and body seemed to be floating around. I could not pin-point what was going on as nothing seemed to help. Several years later, I figured out that I needed to eat gluten free. I wish I had known back then what I know now. The gluten-free diet transformed me physically as well as emotionally. I was not so stressed, irritable or confused. I had much less abdominal pain and stopped losing my hair. I felt sharper and smarter. The benefits of a gluten-free diet have amazed me.

During this tumultuous period with Brittani, Chloe and Toni, I also struggled continuously with my congenital medical condition that effects my immune system, hydration and sodium level. I am vulnerable to stress, which leads me often to question the Lord leading me into such a stressful calling. Fortunately, the Lord has guided me through the process and shown me ways to handle such stress. There have been several times in which I have gone into crisis and almost died as a result of low sodium levels. It is scary to be so vulnerable, but sometimes it is scarier for the ones around you who greatly depend on you. Often, it sent a clear message to our children that I take care of the little things that they do not ever have to think about. I get them where they need to be on time, laundry and dishes are always done as needed rather than piling up, and meals are always on the table, often better than restaurant food. I am appreciated more when I am lying half-dead at the hospital than when I am running around seeing to the variety of chores and duties. There is a comic strip that captures this phenomena:

The comic depicts an older woman sitting in a chair with her feet up when her husband comes home from work. Looking around the room at the children creating messes and climbing on things, he questions her with his eyes and she speaks up, "You know all those times you ask me what I did today? Well, I did not do it."

Similarly, in my times of crisis, everything I am responsible for are brought to light.

Parenting is by far one of the toughest jobs an individual will ever do. Parents understand this, but cannot always pinpoint where their day went. There are several added challenges that adoptive children face. People are generally ignorant of these challenges. The word "typical" is often used to refer to our adoptive child's behavior by people who know little to nothing about traumatized children, i.e. they call it typical teenage behavior. Nothing about our children is typical, but I acquiesce to their assumptions. I half-heartedly agree that it is typical behavior for the age.

I have raised thirteen adopted children and earned a bachelor's degree in sociology, which included child development, sociology, and psychology classes. I am no expert on child development, but I know the difference between normal behavior for their age group and out-of-control, inappropriate behavior. When someone says to me that it sounds like their child's behaviors, a typical child or that it is their age, they devalue not only my intelligence and experience, but my child's past abuses and traumas and insecurities. No one can fully appreciate an adoptive parent's daily struggles until you have lived it.

An adoptive parent becomes saturated after a certain point: like a saturated sponge they are unable to handle any more behavioral problems. When we complain of behaviors, it is difficult to make them sound as bad as they are to live with on a daily basis. The fact that my child steals every chance she gets sounds like I simply need to keep an eye on her better and not allow her to be alone. It is hard to understand what it feels like to be victimized on a daily basis or what it is like to bend over backwards for a child, only to have them immediately steal from you when you turn your back. Interestingly, they often steal when things are going well. We recently had a teenager steal after the family arrived home from eating a $120 restaurant dinner – he shoved a fruit cup in his underwear and ate it while sitting on the toilet.

Seven of our thirteen children have struggled greatly with stealing. Sadly, the stealing always finds its way to Grandma's house or an unsuspecting relative or friend. It is especially difficult on those people. Some people take pity on our kids and emphatically state that it is their age and they will outgrow it, but we have seen where stealing follows them to their adult lives in one way or another, often landing them behind bars. When our children have stolen granola bars, for example, the wrappers never found the garbage. Wrappers are trophies, collected and shoved in baseboard heaters, tub and sink drains, and shirt pockets in their closet. A plate of cookies disappeared, reappearing in the shower. A sandwich disappeared, reappearing two years later behind a large bureau.

The stealing costs money daily and creates a distrust that is not healthy for a parent/child relationship (as well as a potential rodent problem). Lastly, when you watch a child that closely, it means that brushing our teeth, taking a shower, answering the telephone or diverting one's eyes can lead to an opportunity for the child.

We have dealt with many other behaviors beyond stealing: incessant lying when caught red-handed, fire-starting, and inappropriate sexual behaviors. Parents of traumatized children often have a deep longing to be loving, nurturing, normal parents, rather than detectives,

FBI agents, police officers, or corrections officers. We want to talk about how our child's day went at school, rather than why they have another pair of crapped underwear in their drawer with clean underwear, and why they are crapping in their pants at age eleven anyway. We would love to ask them about their first day on their new soccer team, instead of asking about the canteen of urine we found in their closet and the cut up pair of jeans in their dresser with scissors hidden in their pillow case. I would rather get my teeth pulled than point out for the tenth time not to put used women's personal items and bloodied underwear in our bushes outside.

Adoptive parents are human beings, and we have a breaking point. Thankfully, due to our faith in God and the Holy Spirit ministering to us when we cry out, we have endured more than the average person. Amazingly, we are still able to consider further adoptions and we can still smile and hold our head up high, knowing who we are in Christ.

Thankfully, too, our God has guided us to key people in our life who have helped save our family from further destruction. Peggy, an adoptive parent I befriended, bragged about having her two adopted children evaluated by an expert in a nearby state. I had met her a couple of years ago on a whim, a last minute decision to travel states away with my African children to meet other children adopted from the same orphanage. Peggy's excitement was contagious, and she insisted that we, too, get our children tested, even if it meant going into debt. I had previously run across an audio recording of the neuropsychologist while surfing the internet one night. He was explaining adopted children in a way that made sense. While I was listening to the audio recording, I accused him aloud, as if he could hear me, of stealing my words and ideas.

Dr. Ronald S. Federici is a neuropsychologist, as well as an adoptive father of seven. Before meeting him, my greatest fear was that he would do what every other counselor and therapist had done to us, which was judge us and pick apart everything we did wrong while ignoring our child's issues. Our adoptive parent status has made us a prime target for life-long scrutiny. With great anticipation and hesitation, I made an appointment for three of our children to be evaluated by him. He was booking appointments three months out, but that was not a big deal for us because we homeschooled and could then take a week's vacation after public school children were settled into their fall work schedules. Unfortunately, we had to pay for the evaluations with a credit card – we were desperately seeking answers and direction. During the week of testing, he would take a different child each day while the rest of us went to historical sites such as battle grounds, George Washington's homestead and local museums. The last day Dr. Federici conducted a comprehensive overview of each child's test results and a family therapy session. It was refreshing to finally gain an understanding of our children.

Dr. Federici saved our family. He explained how our children ticked. James and I were immediately put at ease by his personable, friendly demeanor as well as his sense of humor. I was mesmerized by his knowledge and understanding. I wanted to stay forever and listen to him. I was excited to have finally found someone who understood my children and could help our family. He was not concerned with what we had done wrong, but focused on what we did right and on our future direction. This is how the foster/adoptive and child protective system should operate, creating solutions instead of focusing solely on blaming. They judge and pre-judge, rather than coming into the situation asking questions with a desire to help us as a family. James and I had learned so much about our children, we needed to process it all. We felt like overfilled balloons, nearly ready to pop. We were anxious to begin our new lives, but leaving Dr. Federici and his support was the most difficult. It was like leaving an uncle. He was now part of our family.

He continued to help us because within a few weeks, we received a full evaluation with several suggestions on how to teach each child, tools to deal with their behaviors and adoptive issues, and what steps to take to help them heal and thrive in our home. He suggested buying therapeutic games like the "Talking, Feeling, Doing Game" and story cards. He gave a list of websites that would address their academic and cognitive shortfalls such as problem solving, logic and memory. He also explained that creating an 'adoption journey' book for each child would help them to put their story together sequentially using words, phrases, stories and pictures. Their books would include the trauma that they have experienced along with the good times. Once complete, their books would sit on the shelf, allowing them to live peacefully, without reliving their trauma. When they wished to look at it, they could take it off the shelf. It differed from a picture album as it was based more on reality than a photo album of happy times together as a family. It would include every family they were a part of or lived with as well as each age. He also demonstrated how to use this homemade adoption journey book and 'reality therapy' to address the root of our children's behaviors and destructive thought patterns.

He explained that our children have organic brain injury from malnutrition, starvation and trauma. Many of our children are able to use very little common sense, logic, reasoning, or communication in any given situation. Most do not understand the difference between unfair treatment and consequences for their behavior. When they respond to reality therapy and Dr. Federici's recommendations, they have more potential. His explanations made sense given the issues we were experiencing with our children and the solutions seemed to point our children back to our family, rather than a variety of service providers.

Dr. Federici explained that traditional talk therapy does not work with traumatized children, but reality therapy uses a unique approach, and since both James and I were well-versed in counseling techniques, we could do this at home. He explained the importance of a strong family unit. Reality therapy is using what is happening or has happened to address their behaviors, thought patterns, made up realities, and post-traumatic stress. Within a few weeks, Josh stopped urinating in his room and the fits of rage ended. Anna spent less time in 'Anna Land' and the children seemed happier than ever. We now had tools to parent our traumatized children more efficiently and effectively. James and I were both amazed at the productivity following one week with someone who understood our family. We had a renewed love and understanding for them and were excited to see them blossoming. Unfortunately, financial difficulties and the continual harassment from the county, took our focus away from fulfilling all of his suggestions to help our children heal. Due to our inability to focus on their healing and the county's harassment and ridicule, our children's mental health and stability plummeted.

And The Walls Came Tumbling Down

With Brittani and Chloe off to college, Toni was the oldest at home. The girls still came home now and then, often with friends. James and I both enjoyed this. We loved being a part of their lives as they became more independent and learned how to make choices on their own.

Brittani began dating a classmate during her first year, despite her Christian college strongly advising against it. The school tried to point out that often a student begins dating and stops making friends. As always, Brittani felt that this was a "stupid rule" and did not apply to her situation. I remember the night she called us after 9:30 pm crying, saying that she was sure she heard from God. She said that God spoke to her heart and told her David was "the one for her to marry." We were so excited that she had heard from God on such an important matter, but we did not know that he and his family would soon replace ours.

Everything seemed to be perfect. We were so proud to have two children in college. We were overjoyed that the transition to college went well. We knew how hardwired their brains were with the insecurities and fears. It was a miracle that they were able to hang on to their adoptive family in a healthy way, while transitioning to college and independence. We loved watching them venture out on their own and listening to their stories about college. Brittani commented that she realized how much we did as a family and how much we traveled. She had talked to her friends at school who did not have the opportunity to travel so much and spend quality time with their families.

During Brittani's second year of college, a sledgehammer hit our family, and it was a sledgehammer we did not see coming. Brittani started being disrespectful to James and me during visits. Chloe was too. At different times, James took each of them to the end of the driveway and drew a line across the width of it. He announced to them that "when they cross that line, they are to be respectful." James also told Brittani that she was not ready for the demands of marriage and should slow her relationship down with David. He explained that she needed to work on her ability to have a healthy give-and-take relationship and her issues of authority and control. About the same time, we began having some major financial difficulties. Between the recession, paying for our third child's braces, and trying to pay the parent's responsibility for two college students, we found ourselves out of money before the two-week pay period ended.

We built up credit card debt bringing Chloe home for much-needed breaks. Chloe began having panic attacks at college and felt she needed her parents and family to help her and support her through this frightening time. We had originally told her that because she was so far away, she would not be going back and forth, but we knew she needed us.

We realized we were struggling financially while Brittani and Chloe could not speak to us respectfully on a consistent basis. We shut Brittani's cell phone off, parked her car and told them that they needed to work part-time or use student loans to pay for the shortfall in their financial aid. We explained our reasoning and struggles to each of them, but Brittani and Chloe were materialistic and could not grasp why we were taking away things that they were entitled to (and all of their friends had). James and I could not keep up anymore and explained that we still loved them, but could not keep paying for everything like we had been, especially when they could not be consistently respectful. We could not eat meat anymore, because it was too expensive. We could not buy sneakers when they were worn out. We used the credit card for basic necessities such as groceries. It was the beginning of a train wreck. The sledgehammer began to come down hard when the money, car and cell phone were taken away.

Meanwhile, we were unaware of what was going on behind the scenes. There was a traitor among us, who was attempting to destroy the family. Toni was still at home, a teenager now. She was going to church youth group leaders and other organizational leaders and spewing garbage about alleged difficulties at home. She had a great relationship with us, which involved the typical give-and-take between parents and teenagers, so her alleged difficulties were completely fabricated for dramatic effect. We were unaware of the lies she was spreading, because when she was in front of us she spoke kindly and respectfully most of the time, and seemed to make sense when she would hash things out with us regarding school, her future, life and problems. Unbeknownst to us, she was instigating to get Brittani, Chloe and the church leaders angry and upset with us, i.e. telling them that we did not let her do anything outside of the home with friends, that Josh was treated poorly because of the gluten, sugar and dairy-free diets we were trying with him, and that we unfairly favored Rebekka over Toni (the lies are too numerous to recount here).

It was like being in a movie where the informant is not who you think it is. You watch the movie thinking you know who the bad guys are, but it seems odd that the bad guys always know everything, things they would not normally know. They seem to always be there. They seem to always know things and no one knows where the 'leak' is. Toward the end of the movie, you realize it was someone on the inside, informing them of the investigation and planned raids. It felt like that in our home.

We did not know what was going on, but people seemed to have twisted ideas and would make odd comments. We were being viewed through lenses created by Toni's lies. It was creepy. We were always watching our backs. It felt like people were analyzing and watching our every move. With this type of pressure, it makes it difficult to be yourself and enjoy your children and your spouse. We were being oppressed.

Meanwhile, we were allowing Toni to go to Scotland on a mission's trip, and attend weekly youth group meetings, community college classes, dance class, weekly meetings of a teen advocacy program, including its special activities held at local hotels, amusement parks and theatres. Amazingly, she was complaining that she did not get to do anything, while I ran her from one place to another on a daily basis. No one looked at reality and saw that she was going several places without us and doing many different activities.

She told people that we would not allow her go to Brittani's wedding, even though we were never told when or where it was, and she never asked. She told us that she had no desire to go, but ought to go because people would be there that she would like to see. We supported her decision and agreed to get her there if her final decision was to go. We thought we were having meaningful heart to heart talks with her, helping her come to peace with her decision, but meanwhile, she was telling people something completely different.

Brittani also told everyone at her wedding that we did not want to go. We were never invited. Toni loved to play both sides and she had mastered the art; people at church believed her, even when the evidence plainly showed otherwise. We were very open about what went on in our family to lessen the impact of Toni's lies. To this day, we still shake our heads in disbelief about how ignorant and naïve our fellow "adult" church members were about how manipulative an adoptive teen can be. We had spent countless hours trying to educate them for four years about the unique challenges our adoptive family faced and yet when Toni acted just as we predicted, they were completely manipulated by lies and forgot or ignored everything we said. We had no credibility despite the fact that we had 13 adopted children. I had an organization leader tell me that she checked out a couple of her tales and found out that they were lies, but was not sure if the other things she said about us were lies. For some reason, they all gave credit to Toni's fabricated reality and blamed us for her difficulties, while ignoring the overarching power of her childhood traumas. Her trauma was completely ignored. Unfortunately, given many of our children's manipulative behaviors, the phrase, "It takes a whole village to raise a child," is an opportunity for them to manipulate and create a 'team of people' against their family and their family's rules. Toni used this to her full advantage, with people we had known and trusted. Social media is her favorite venue for her manipulation, inner anger and confusion. Her feelings of rejection, insecurity, and unworthiness are paramount in the way she manipulates.

Not surprisingly, we were hit with another round of abuse allegations during this time. Toni had been defiant and disrespectful following the holidays. She was acting odd. She was trying to make us angry and trying to make us say or do something, but we refused to bite. James and I both tried to reason with her and talk to her, while she continued to bait us. We were confused, but we knew something was fishy. One thing that James and I have learned, is that if it smells like fish, it is fish.

Dedra called me out of the blue with an elaborate story about having Toni over for the weekend to visit with her daughter, whom Toni considered a big sister. I melted and, like always, I forgot how disrespectful she had been acting all week. I always melted with compassion when there was any type of reunion or visit with a previous family. I understand how much these children had already connected with people before we came into their lives and believe in maintaining those ties. I never wanted to be the one who held them back from relationships with people whom they cared deeply about, even if they were not as healthy for them as I would like. I never felt threatened by their previous relationships. They were a part of my children.

Toni's relationship with Dedra was not ideal. She had a twisted relationship with Toni, but we felt that if we could combat her twisted ideas with reality, Toni would see Dedra for who she was and love her despite these twisted beliefs. Our compassion blew up in our face.

Dedra started repeatedly telling Toni that we stole her and that we kept her away from Dedra. Dedra was dead wrong. We had initiated visits, called Dedra, encouraged respect for Dedra, and drove Toni back and forth to visit with her. Dedra did nothing to maintain the relationship. This was the first time Dedra had called us.

James and I work as a team. We consult one another before making decisions. He has the discernment and I have the unbridled compassion. He has the level head and I am guided by emotion. He has the memory and I have no memory. So, we bounce things off of each other before making decisions. However, this time I went with my compassion and forgetful forgiveness and allowed Toni to go to Dedra's house despite her odd and defiant behavior. It would be a mistake that would nearly cost us our family.

Toni had been gone all day with an adult church friend whom we trusted. She was a leader of an advocacy organization Toni was involved in. With Toni's homeschool hours being so flexible, she was able to meet with senators and government officials on behalf of the organization during the week when public school children could not. I allowed this as long as Toni got her school work done. I also considered much of these experiences as a good education for her. She was learning about public speaking, government, planning and writing. This group seemed to be good for her and good for a resume later on.

We did not know at the time that the Christian adults we trusted with our daughter were filling her head with undermining ideas and helping her be sneaky. For example, Toni was excited about her decision to join the Marines after graduation. One of the male leaders of this organization told her that she should not go into the Marines because she would get shot and killed. He told her that she should go to college, even though college was not a realistic option for Toni at that time. She did not have the discipline or ability to follow through with her classes. After paying for several college classes, we learned that she had no intention in following through with joining the Marines.

We also did not know at the time, that the Christian adults we trusted were in on the most destructive plan James and I could ever imagine. Toni orchestrated this entire weekend at Dedra's from the organization leader's cell phone, and following this weekend, our family would never be the same.

When Toni came home from the all-day session with the leader of the organization, Toni was intent on getting ready to leave. I was chasing her down to tell her about Dedra's phone call and that Dedra would be here to pick her up any minute. It was the first time Dedra facilitated a visit with Toni in the 12 years she had known us and we should have known something was not right.

Toni's big sister, Brittani was also calling her after a year of silence.

When I told Brittani that Toni was not here, she said, "Yeah right."

"When have I ever lied to you?" I asked. I felt stabs in my chest. She made a disrespectful noise and I hung up the telephone.

I was intent on explaining to Toni what was going on. I did not realize Toni had already planned to leave, before I told her. She already knew Dedra was coming to get her. I should have been alerted. I also wanted to prepare Toni for Brittani's rampage. I wanted Toni to stand up for what she believed in, rather than succumb to Brittani's anger and intimidation.

Looking back now, I feel stupid for being so naïve, but in some ways, I think God protects us from the truth because it would have been ugly had I told Toni she could not go. Dedra and Toni would have made it disastrous and would have made it look like I got angry and did something to Toni I did not do. That is how they operate. To let Toni out the door peacefully and smiling, was surely the best thing to do.

The next day, I called Dedra to tell her I was picking Toni up in an hour. Dedra pitched a fit, telling me she never got to see her daughter because of the snowstorm and that she needed to stay. This was uncharacteristic for Dedra. James and I sensed that Toni needed to come home immediately. Dedra then informed me that Toni visited with Brittani. My heart sank. I was not sure what Dedra was up to, but I did not like it. Brittani has been allowed to contact our children at our house anytime she wished, but has not. Brittani has completely shut us and our children out of her life. Brittani does not like Dedra, at all. This made no sense. Warning bells were ringing loudly at this point. Brittani had not had anything good to say about us for a year, ever since she started dating her boyfriend. There was a time when Brittani called crying and asking for forgiveness, asking if she could call the children once a week on Friday. I was overjoyed and told her I would love it if she did. The kids missed their big sister. She called for three weeks on Fridays and we never heard from her again. When she ditched us, she ditched her younger brother and sisters, her grandparents, great grandparents, aunts, uncles and many friends as well as their memories. Unfortunately, I see this as a pattern in her life and the pattern will continue if she does not recognize it and take steps to stop this destructive pattern.

Picking up Toni at Dedra's that weekend was an adventure. It was like walking into the twilight zone. I felt lost and drunk with confusion. It was as if I had walked out on a stage during a play, and was an actor without the script. I was scared to be in her house. I wanted to get out as soon as possible, but her older daughter was blocking the door. Dedra was hugging Toni like Toni's dog just died, saying that everything will be alright and if she needed anything, let her know. Then the older daughter and her boyfriend whom Toni was supposedly going to see, chimed in with similar statements. I had no idea what they were alluding to. When we walked out the door, I asked Toni about the odd comments and she pled innocence and said she had no idea. I knew she did, but she lies as well as her teacher, Dedra. It is never any use to push the matter.

We sat Toni down to talk to her when she got home. We were concerned that the visit with Brittani would confuse Toni. We wanted to help her process the visit and what transpired. We wanted to help her untwist her thoughts because we know Brittani is a crazy-maker. Brittani's perception of our family was not based on reality, and we were focusing on reality therapy and showing Toni that we are there for her and care for her.

We knew that Brittani's wedding was fast approaching. We were not allowed to know when it was or where it was, but it was easy for James to figure it out. He deduces things easily. It is part of who he is. We assumed Brittani would try to confuse things and intimidate Toni to participate in something she did not want to participate in. Until now, Toni had not expressed an interest in Brittani's wedding plans. We offered to take her or to get her a ride to the wedding. We wanted Toni to be part of Brittani's wedding if there was any part of her that would later regret not going. But on the other hand, we did not want Toni to feel obligated to go. We wanted Toni to make a level-headed decision, but she had too many lies swimming around her head. Our common sense and logic was convoluted by others' nonsensical comments about us not allowing her to go and Brittani's desire to not invite us.

Brittani's wedding was a big secret. Brittani told Toni to sneak out of the house and steal a ride in the night if she wanted to go. It was a shame people, especially her sister and church friends, encouraged her to run away. The same people we encouraged our children to be respectful to all these years, did not return the same courtesy.

Brittani and Chloe had been the same way when they were teenagers. It was all about survival without the parents knowing what they were thinking. We were not worthy of knowing what they were thinking so that we could help them through their troubles. However, there were times when James could get Brittani talking; he spent hours trying to untwist her perceptions of life and our family and anything on her mind. The only time I ever got through to her was when I wrote a Valentine's note to her - it seemed to temporarily resolve her inner confusion and anger. She ended up crying, writing me a note back and apologizing whole-heartedly for her actions and words. These moments stick out to me today, as I see a miserable, mean-spirited young adult. Inside she is still the sad, hurting, eight-year-old child, standing on the porch of her foster home, waiting for James to pick her up for her new adoptive home.

A week after we picked Toni up at Dedra's, we had two unwelcome visitors at the door. It was child protective services. They come in pairs when they tell you about the allegations of abuse in case you become violent or angry. I was not either one. It hurts more than anything. It hurt that Brittani and Chloe would be so cruel as to do something to jeopardize our family's unity, security and happiness, especially when they had experienced such insecurities in their early childhood.

Why would they want their younger adopted siblings from an overseas orphanage (and a private adoption) to experience the same heartaches, rejection, constant transitions, and insecurities that they had gone through in foster care as young children? The children in our home were ages 5, 9, 11, 12, 14 and 16. What did we do that was so bad that our children needed to be pulled out of our home and placed in a foster home they did not know rather than remain with us? Did Brittani really want Dawson and Samuel to be placed in a foster home? What if it was not a good foster home? What if we had never gotten them back again? Is that really what she wanted for them? It killed us inside. It sickens me and I keep thinking that someday it is going to be their children if they are not careful with how they treat others.

We did not know all the details, but we knew it must have been the Dedra, Toni and Brittani alliance, which was forged to destroy our family. They alleged we were inappropriately disciplining them. Thankfully, the assigned case worker saw that Brittani acted a bit crazy and did not seem believable. Because it was me (and I was a long-time designee on the County's blacklist), there was a full investigation that lasted well beyond the sixty days they are allotted to investigate. The case worker was also told by her supervisor to conduct several unannounced visits. Each time she came, the visit disrupted and upset the children and left us all feeling awkward and violated. When parents need to be checked on, it sends the wrong signals to the children and creates unwarranted insecurity and fear. Our children had been through so much that I hated to see them have to go through this nonsense, but soon it would be over and we could go on with our lives. Or would it?

During the investigation, Brittani called the case worker twice a week to ask why our children were still in the home and why she was not placing them in foster care. The case worker was young and inexperienced with no children, so she unfortunately gave Brittani an audience. The case worker explained to Brittani that it takes more than one allegation to remove children from a home. I initially panicked when I heard this. I knew this would merely give Brittani a license to fabricate additional allegations. I knew Brittani and her allies would up the ante in order to accomplish their ultimate goal, and I told this young inexperienced case worker this. She stared blankly at me – she was clueless. James and I suspected that Brittani had an underlying motive to take our children into her home.

As with Jesslyn, Toni had never been doing better in our home than at the time she turned on us. We have learned that many traumatized children cannot accept success and will demolish their accomplishments. She was happy. She had asked for some new clothing and personal items, all of which I bought for her. Later on, I realized that this was a pattern and has become her calling card. She sees what she can get you to buy her, before she leaves, without the items. She was fully engaged in the teenage advocacy organization and had just participated in a weekend-long filming of a feature to be distributed to government and media industry leaders. She was in dance and youth group. She also had a job that accentuated her talents. Her job was second in command at a nearby museum and small store. She had a computer to use and books to read to keep her busy during down-time. Everyone loved her. She was a high school senior and was taking two classes at a local community college. She was continuously bragging on the way home that she answered questions no one else could answer. She liked a guy at college whom we invited to go with us to a comedian show.

We sacrificed our time and money to get her ready for a successful transition to independence. I was excited for her progress and her growing self-confidence. James and I were so proud of her. I had signed her up to participate in the home school graduation ceremony coming up. She then planned to enter the military after completing enough college credits to get into the branch she wanted. She was seriously considering the military police, which Brittani had originally wanted to do but could not due to her allergy to bees. James and I knew that she may not decide to follow through with that, but we encouraged her, "at least it is a goal to aspire to." James and I believe in goals. Goals help you move forward in life and not become too stagnant.

The Accomplice

Each passing day, we found out more of who was behind the cruel plot. Having Toni in our home became dangerous to our family, but there was nothing we could do legally. We were left to continue to play our parts in her play. It was hurtful to know that Brittani and Toni would stoop so low and become so cruel- hearted. We had done everything for them, but Toni did not care who she hurt along the way to get to where she wanted to go. People were simply pawns in her game of life, pawns to manipulate and win. They did not realize that pushing away the only people that ever cared about you was not winning. It is one thing to decide not to be part of a family and to disown your family, but they did not need to destroy us on their way out.

There were numerous people involved in this hurtful conspiracy. One by one, it came to our attention that someone else we had thought was a good friend in reality was not. It was sad and more hurtful than I had ever experienced. I could not understand why people could not see reality, but instead believed the girls' slander, and why no one we had considered a good friend confronted us about what our girls were saying behind our backs. We found out that Brittani stayed overnight at a friend's house while coordinating the meeting with Toni and the trip to child protective. This particular friend was also a worker in our church's children's program. We had gone to church the week before, not knowing about this upcoming abuse allegation. How many weeks had this children's program worker known that we were going to be stabbed in the back by our daughter? It was embarrassing.

When I tried to talk to the pastor about what we were going through, he walked away while I was talking. I was astonished that he did not seem disturbed, sad for us, concerned, or offer prayer for our situation, or even finish listening to me. Now I know that he and his wife were part of it all, too.

The year before the abuse allegations, Chloe insisted on coming home for the summer. I drove 16 hours to go pick her up. I explained to her that she needed to be respectful. She agreed and hugged me like she was never going to let me go. James and I helped her get a job at a burger joint nearby and surprised her with fixing the extra car and putting it on the road.

The first week was so exciting; I missed her and loved having her home again. After the first week, she suddenly started hibernating in her room, sitting on the computer for hours upon hours, and acting weird about us touching her little dog she'd brought home. We did not know at the time what had changed her, but she became mean and withdrawn. One day, she used the car to go to the pastor's house for dinner. She ended up spending her time with them complaining about us and how Toni did not get to do anything and that we did not do anything for her. The pastor and his wife offered her a place to stay. This is the worst thing that someone can say to a traumatized adoptive child – once they have an out, they will throw their family away. When Chloe's disrespect increased and she screamed at us that the pastor invited her to live with them, James explained to the pastor that he was wrong, and it changed our relationship with the church forever.

We had hoped the pastor would have come to us first to ask us if Chloe could stay there or ask us if there was really a problem in our home. The right thing to do would have been to offer us help. If there was any concern about us as parents, it seems that a pastor would approach us, counsel us, and rehabilitate us, if you will. Nothing more was said. Over the years, we have seen it time and time again where others see adoptive children as "free agents" who need parents. They will not respect your role as an adoptive parent. If you are an adoptive parent, you need to safeguard your children against other adults, who will repeatedly try to speak into your children's lives – even though they have no business doing so. Adoptive children have parents!

Chloe decided to go back to her college town and planned to live with a friend. She did not like the rules the Pastor and his wife set down before her. She spent the entire 16-hour ride to her college town screaming at me in the car and at each stop. I reached out for the dog and insisted I could watch her little dog at a rest area, so she could go to the bathroom. She nearly choked the dog, pulling away from me, and blamed me for choking it as she screamed to the top of her lungs and then refused to go to the bathroom the entire trip. I tried to iron things out with her in the middle of the trip at a rest area, coaxing her to use the facilities, and calmly, quietly talking to her. She immediately began screaming again. I planned to wait it out and speak truth, but got scared that others might hear and send authorities after my vehicle, so I sped off nervously. She stopped screaming long enough to eat the food I bought on the way. I handed it to her and said, "Here, eat some, I bought plenty. After all, it is not me with the problem, it is you. I do not have a problem with you and I did not want you to leave."

A month after the allegation, James and I began to realize how two-faced our daughter, Toni was. For years, we wanted to see the good in her and not focus on her faults. We wanted the best for her and not to limit her. We wanted her to keep striving for more and not settle with a mediocre lifestyle where people often feel stuck. We wanted her to be happy. Those were our dreams for her life, not hers. Her dreams were small. She wanted to be running the streets with other teenagers and have children. It became apparent that Toni had manipulated Brittani and had been telling her stories. Toni wanted complete freedom to do whatever she wanted and we were hindering her from fulfilling that desire, or in her case that need.

A few weeks after the allegation, Toni came to me and told me that she wanted to call the case worker and tell her she had made it all up. I explained to Toni that she had already gotten the ball rolling and it had to run its course, but if she felt the need to call, she could certainly do that. I gave her the card with the case workers 'phone number on it and walked away calmly. Apparently, she followed through. She called the case worker and rescinded her abuse allegations, but the case worker told her exactly what I had told her. Her comments now were of no use; an investigation had been launched. It did not matter if the accuser told them it was all a lie. Part of me wonders if there is a kind, calm, sweet person inside Toni and she is like Dr. Jekyll and Mr. Hyde, or if everything she says and does is manipulative. I know that she wanted us to believe she was taking it all back because her plan for freeing herself from the family was not working out as Dedra, Brittani and Toni had planned. I know in Dedra's mind, she was supposed to get custody of Toni. That is why Dedra did not want me to pick her up that weekend before child protective showed up.

Despite everything, we allowed Toni to attend Brittani's wedding. James sat in the car outside the reception hall, as an unwanted guest, eating McDonald's food. It was humiliating for a father of an adoptive daughter whom he once held a close bond with. It broke his heart and mine too. Waiting at home, I was reminded of our trip to Africa together and the opportunity to preach at a local university. I could see people responding to my message, but when Brittani began to speak directly from her heart everyone was completely engaged. As I looked around the open aired hut, I saw tears streaming down grown men's cheeks. I saw my daughter open up in a way I had never seen before, speaking of adoption as being a life-saving event for her, but moreover, a relationship with Jesus was necessary for a fulfilled life. Brittani never cried in front of anyone, let alone a hundred or so strangers. I was in awe – her message and emotion was impressive. My heart glowed and I was overwhelmed with happiness and pride. Only months later, we are uninvited and unwanted guests at her wedding. James was not walking her down the aisle to her future husband, but sitting in a hot stuffy car eating fast food. I found it odd that not one of those guests who truly new our hearts would remind her how much we did for her, how happy she was growing up and how much we obviously loved her; but they had all been lied to. As far as they knew, we did not want to be there.

Following the wedding, Toni's behavior changed. She went from being sweet and happy after having been forgiven, to once again, being completely defiant and mean-spirited. She went out of her way to be nasty. For example, she rolled her eyes and mumbled under her breath every time we said something. She also started picking fights with the younger children. I could tell that she was again trying to make me say or do something that she could use against me. I remained calm and fair.

One day, I received an alert from the library that our books were due, but in that alert was a magazine I did not recognize as ours. I knew it must have been Toni's. She liked those magazines, but I had asked her if she could concentrate on her college classes, her job, and her school classes until college breaks and then take books and magazines out for leisurely reading. It was not a demand, but just a strong recommendation because I felt she was busy enough and was naturally scatter-brained. In response, Toni did what she always does when given a rule. She acted like she agreed and understood, while she did as she pleased behind our backs. When I confronted her about the magazine, I told her I was not angry and I understood that perhaps she needed something relaxing to read, but I needed to know where it was, because it was due. She denied knowing anything about it or where it was. I asked again, explaining that I did not care but needed to know because we would have to pay overdue fines. She continued to deny any knowledge of it, while I began to look for it. I found it in her bag in the closet. I was relieved and walked away to the pile of books from the library. She was disgusted that I had found it, and disgusted that she had been caught. In her upset, she spun around quickly, tossing her head to the side, rolling her eyes at me, and accidentally smashed into the open closet door. I was beside her. She looked at me as if I had done it to her, causing her blackened, puffy eye. I looked at her, as if to say, "Don't you dare blame that on me."

Later, I found a picture of that black eye on her camera as if she planned on using it against me. She had also taken pictures of other random injuries she had gotten from various sources. It was scary to look at, but what I found on the computer was scarier. In the recycle bin of my computer was my daughter Toni taking selfies of herself completely in the nude. It was embarrassing for me to look at, but I was grateful it was I who found it rather than one of my kids or my husband. What worried my husband and I most, was why she downloaded these pictures and who they went to.

She eventually lost her patience because we refused to take the bait. She upped the ante by randomly refusing to get into the car for soccer. She loved soccer so it was hurting her, as well as everyone else. I did not dare leave her home alone with her acting crazy so we all stayed home. She then began listening to her stereo loudly. I walked up to her room and calmly stated that she was not going to get to listen to her music if she refused to go to soccer practice. Looking back, I probably should have allowed her to play her power trip and ignored it completely, but I felt for the other children who were forced to stay home. She yelled at me and continued to play her stereo. I threatened to take it out of there, and she threatened to get violent. I stated that I would call the police if I had to. She then announced that I had hurt her hand, and if I called the police, she would tell them I hurt her. I smiled and told her I was not afraid of her lies and threats.

I unplugged her stereo and took it out of her room. Unfortunately, I had to put it down on the steps because I was losing my grip. In her anger, Toni drop-kicked it into my face, nearly causing me to lose my balance and fall backwards down the flight of stairs. To think about that, years later, scares me. I could have gotten seriously hurt if I had fallen backward. Without emotion, I proceeded to carry it downstairs, at this point, not caring that she had broken it. Despite my best efforts to appear calm, my heart was beating and my body was in flight-or-fight mode. I was not intimidated by her, but I also knew that she would do anything to provoke me and she would do anything to hurt herself and then turn around and say that I attacked her. She was getting desperate to move on with her life. She was unsatisfied with her college classes, cushy job, and family life. She was like a cat in heat. You cannot keep a cat like that in the house. They will run out of the smallest opening. Toni was in search of that open door. We had been through this before with Jesslyn and Miguel. When a traumatized child is finished with your home, they do not rest until they destroy their relationship with the family. Reality therapy can head it off at the pass, if they allow it to sink in, but she clearly had already made a decision.

I alerted James of her desperate measures to get us into trouble. It finally came to a head after weeks of this behavior. A couple of days after Father's Day, Toni was on day three of giving us the silent treatment. We had a simple rule that you let people in the house know when you are headed into the shower because it means that our only bathroom would be occupied for a while. Of course, Toni buzzed past everyone to take a shower without saying a word. James called her out of the bathroom - she had not shut the door behind her yet, as if she was expecting to be spoken to. He told her that her continued disrespect was unnecessary and was not going to be tolerated any longer. He told her that she needed to help around the house like everyone else. He also exposed some of her lies and manipulation techniques used during the past few months. I chimed in and told her that we knew she was purposely not doing her homework for her college classes, even though at one point, she had been excited about the classes, as well as the homework assigned. The homework was fun and thought-provoking. She would share many of the assignments with us as she did them. James continued to point out facts and contradictions in her behavior and after about twenty minutes of it, walked away, telling her to take her shower. I could see in Toni's eyes; she was not finished. Most of the time, these talks would alter her behavior at least for a day or so. This time it did nothing, but make Toni's eyes more set on harming us.

After Toni's shower, she went upstairs and down and out through a back stairway. We knew she was going to do something like that, but for some reason, we did not take precautions. We had a security system we could have set, but instead, James read a bedtime story to the children and I was copying papers. She had poor judgment, so we scoured the woods and fields and roads for hours. I stopped looking at three o'clock in the morning and James stopped at six o'clock in the morning. We were afraid that she might hurt herself inadvertently or be picked up by someone who was untrustworthy. We had shady characters living in our area.

We did not find out until three o'clock in the afternoon the next day that Toni was fine and had been in a safe home for abused individuals since the night before at eleven o'clock (only an hour after she left our home). I was furious that we were not told she was safe until 14 hours later. James missed a day of work, and we were both concerned about Toni's safety. Regardless of the tales she told them about us, we deserved to know that she was safe.

Child protective came to our house again. Not surprisingly, Toni had gone to our most untrustworthy neighbor with the shadiest character when she ran away. From there, she went to a safe house. The allegations would have been amusing if it had not been our reputation, family and freedom in jeopardy. The allegations stated that James had slammed Toni's head against the wall repeatedly before she ran away. It also said something about her having a bloody nose when she left. She had no bloody nose, although they were common for her. If child protective and the safe house had thought Toni was telling the truth, James and I were confused as to why they did not bring her to an emergency room to check her out and get X-rays or a CT scan. Instead, she went to Jadin's house to stay the weekend. I told Jadin that he did not have to take her in. I warned him of her tactics. Well, a weekend turned into nine months. He did not heed our warnings, so he got to fully experience her manipulative behavior.

The Allegations and Investigation

Allegations of abuse seem harmless enough to the under-educated adoptive family. In a fair and just environment, a family is accused of some type of horrendous deed, considered innocent until investigated thoroughly in an objectively respectful manner by professionals in the field, and either given the help they need to become better parents or given a letter of reprieve. In dangerous situations, the children should be taken away from the parents until they get the help they need. Adoptive families often mistakenly view the child protective services system this way the first time allegations are made against them. The family tends to be upset, but open up their home for investigation as they have nothing to hide. Unfortunately, this is not how it operates. Child protective workers assume you are guilty before proven innocent. When they enter your home, they immediately look for anything that slightly supports the allegations and your guilt.

Toni's allegations were preposterous. The allegations did not make sense. This was the second time she turned us in for abuse within months, and the first one, she recanted. However, the accuser's credibility is not typically scrutinized, only the accused. Toni alleged that James slammed her head against the wall several times. James merely spoke firmly, but Toni did not want to hear any truth about her immature behavior. I pointed to the place where they both stood and because there was a wall in the vicinity, the case worker's eyes lit up. It was immediately written down and became fact that James indeed slammed her head against the wall several times. I noticed the child protective worker writing feverishly as I pointed to the place. I knew what I had done. Anything that gave them what they needed to prove that we were guilty, they immediately wrote down. Anything that disproved our guilt and portrayed our innocence, was passed by.

Unfortunately, it is upsetting when these workers come in like lions and barely listen to what you have to say, and for some reason, I could not shake this off. I was an emotional mess that day. I could not stop crying. I cried for Toni and her destructive patterns. I cried for our reputation being marred once again by a troubled teen who did not understand the implications of what she was doing. I cried for my children who did not deserve this trauma added to their uncertain lives. I cried for the system for being so mean and cruel and unfair. I cried because I needed my mom who was dying of cancer. I cried because I am a parent and I care about my children. I cried because these people who barged into our home assumed the worst and deemed us guilty without giving us a fair investigation or benefit of the doubt. I cried for my children who had to now undergo an interrogation that they did not understand or have the ability to answer such loaded questions. One wrong stare or confusion or word could result in prison for us or foster care for our children, or both.

Our children were already traumatized from a past life. They do not answer questions the way a non-traumatized child would. They give "deer in the headlights" looks when asked the simplest questions. They get confused easily because their stress level goes up higher and faster than most children. Their eyes bounce around in fear and distress, which to the untrained eye would make them look like liars. They do not understand certain terminology an American born child would understand, such as: over, under, behind, in front of, before, after or above. They do not know American slang and idioms, even though we use them often. They do not know how to communicate effectively, and many of our children struggled with language deficits and cognitive impairment from malnutrition on top of all that.

The investigation was a train wreck. Like I said, I was an upset mess, and I should never have allowed them in our home until I could pull myself together emotionally. The workers were two hours late for their appointment at our house. I had finally given up, and let the dogs out of their crate to go outside. Of course, that is when child protective showed up. They asked that I put the dogs away because one of the

195

workers was deathly afraid of the dogs. I explained that the one dog was old and did not care about them. I also told them that they were two hours late, and the dogs had suffered enough for them. I left them out. The workers then had a problem with the fact that I told them they were not talking to my children alone. I explained that we had had the sexual abuse task force speak to our older children alone when they were younger, and it completely traumatized them. The one young lady had worn a low-cut shirt and kept bending over the table to ask my children a question while they looked down her shirt at her nearly fully-exposed boobs. In this interview years ago, my daughter had been asked if she had ever been sexually abused by her father. She stared in her traumatized fear and memories. She did not know what to say, and it destroyed her emotionally. She explained to me later that she did not know what to say because her birth father had sexually abused her, but not her adoptive father. I hugged her and told her it was okay that she got confused and scared and could not answer. I told her I was so sorry for allowing them to talk to her without me in the room. She is now in her twenties and still lives with the effects of being sexually abused and traumatized at such a young age by her birth parents. Being questioned alone by insensitive, clueless child protective workers only exacerbated the trauma.

After the lengthy explanation of my concerns, the case workers standing on my porch, had no emotion and were only concerned about their investigation, not my children. They immediately called their supervisor to ask if it was acceptable that I was in the room. After several minutes on the phone, the case worker compromised and allowed me to sit in the adjoining room during the investigation. Each child was questioned separately.

Amidst the tragedy of the investigation and situation we were in, I could not help but love my children more and smile as they answered each question to the best of their ability. To the child protective worker, it was a game to get the child to say something she could use against us. To me, the parent, it was an opportunity to see their individual personalities and mannerisms shine through. It was adorable. I wanted to hug each child as they sat on the hot seat being interrogated by two strangers. I wanted to save them. A parent's job is to keep them safe and secure, but when child protective is involved, it is no longer our choice. We are left on the sidelines and are powerless to protect our children. It is scary and sad, especially when these workers have less education and experience than I do in the area of human services, sociology, trauma, adoption, foster care, abused children, neglected children and communication techniques. They do not know our children and do not care to get to know them. Most of these workers do not have children, much less ever experienced a foster or adoptive child with childhood trauma scarring their personalities and perceptions of life. These interviews are devastating to the children. Traumatized children are hypersensitive to change, trauma, and new people. They also struggle with indiscriminate attachments.

Our six-year-old took this opportunity to have fun, a decision which would later cause him great sadness and shame. He loves attention and can tell tall tales. I decided long ago he would not darken the doors of a public school. He loves to babble to anyone willing to listen. This was his arena. He had two pretty young women not much older than he, hanging on every word he said. He was in his glory. His excitement showed in his voice. He immediately talked about looking out the window while Toni was getting yelled at and watching the birds. Anyone with half a brain would have caught that as odd because it was 9 pm and birds are not out at night, nor can you see them because the lights are on in the house when it is dark outside and you see nothing but your reflection. He then talked about some other nonsense I did not understand, but the next thing he said, would turn the tables.

He reiterated the allegation word for word. To an experienced parent or child worker, that would be a red flag that he was lying. Children at age six do not use the same words to describe things as adults. He had heard me tell my dying mother about the abuse allegations and therefore, thought he knew what had happened that night. He had no idea what he was doing. He was having fun with two people that were willing to listen to him. He went on to talk about there being blood all over the place. I tried to stop him with the intent to refocus him and remind him that he is supposed to be telling her what he saw or heard, and not make up things or repeat what he heard me tell my mother. He would not stop telling his imaginative story. He was a young boy and loved the idea of blood and gore.

I sat down defeated, knowing what it would do to their investigation. They had all they needed now. They could stop their investigation right there, and they did, other than looking at our house and allowing my son to continue in his foolish talk. He began to ramble on and on about something I did not understand. His story was a mixture of the Lion King and Star Trek occasionally mentioning our names as characters. He was not making any sense. I was secretly hoping the case worker had written all that he said, but I was sure she only wrote what she needed him to say. Finally, one of the girls asked me what he was talking about. I was barely paying attention because he had lost me in his elaborate details, and I refocused and said, "I do not know. Nothing he has said has made any sense. It has all been made up. I cannot help you." She asked again, if it was from a book he read, like the "Lion King." I reiterated that I had no idea and that I did not understand what he was talking about at all. I was frustrated, not at my son, but at the young fools that were only catching the words they needed to hear, to use against us. I was not angry at my son, but they glared at me uneasily each time I had any interaction with him after that, as if they feared I would retaliate against the whistleblower.

When it was my turn to be questioned, the caseworkers asked me questions like a machine gun, not giving me time to answer the first question, before asking the next question. As I continued to answer the first question, they would "get confused" and ask ignorant questions as if I was answering the second question and my answer was not making sense to them. They were attempting to fluster and confuse me, rather than seek the truth. I held steadfast and answered only one question at a time, but they acted as if my answer was not making any sense because it was not what they had asked. I knew I was in trouble because that was a sign that they had already made up their minds, and now they were simply looking for more information to add to their report such as, "Mother became flustered…" They never did listen to the answer to any of their questions. Then they had to leave because it was getting to be 4:30, which is the end of their work day. I have seen rooms at the county building clear out at 4:30 without any announcements or good-byes during a meeting with people in the middle of a sentence.

Days later, when I was able to pull myself together emotionally, and was able to stop crying and able to think clearly, this whole scenario disgusted me. Toni claimed to have been slammed up against the wall several times. Toni, being about 120 pounds and her father being about 207 pounds, it seems the runaway shelter would have sense enough to have her checked at an emergency room, but she was never brought to one. Toni also claimed that she had a bloody nose and yet she never accused James of touching her face, only slamming her head. There were no drops of blood in her room on the carpet or any type of trail or spots or bloodied tissue in the garbage. Later, Toni claimed that she only used a washcloth at our neighbor's house because she had pimples that popped. Also, where Toni stood as James lectured her, there was a nail in the wall. That nail was at Toni's height and would have done damage to her head, had it been slammed against the wall, not to mention the wall would have been dented or cracked. Our walls are almost 120 years old. They probably would not take to slamming a head into them too many times. Jadin, whom she went to stay with directly after the incident, made a statement to child protective that Toni was fine the next day and appeared to have no lasting effects from the night before. She complained of no headache or pain and she was happy and smiling and playing with his son. This statement was never recorded in the records, which angered Jadin.

A few days later I was scheduled to meet a domestic violence worker at his office. Before our meeting, I made it clear that I did not want my young children listening to the conversation. As I approached the room they chose to use for the meeting, there was another seasoned worker as well as the young man whom I had spoken to. The older worker jumped immediately into the topic at hand. I did not force the issue that my children should be in another room. I do not know if I was intimidated or I felt that it would not be too personal, or I wanted them with me and did not trust anyone to be with them. Later, my children complained that it was difficult for them to sit there while I was being treated so meanly. The woman seemed to listen to what I had to say, unlike the workers that came into my home, but it was only a way to get more information and jump on everything I said. I found myself reaching, trying desperately to explain our position on things, as well as Toni's personality. I explained Toni's personality and what brought her to a place like this and was in turn asked how I could still love her. I looked perplexed at the woman and said, "I am her Mom. Mother's love their children where they are at. I understand her and know her, but I still love her."

It was such a confusing meeting. The young man played no role in the meeting, whereas the older woman ran the show. She had me spinning around and chasing my tail. She accused me of sending my 16-year-old to college classes. I explained that it was two college classes, which were designed for high school seniors. I explained that she enjoyed them and answered the first question asked in class. She was proud of herself as no one knew the answer. I was amazed that this woman was painting a negative picture of someone attending college courses. I could not untwist this reasoning. She then attacked Dr. Federici's evaluation of Toni. I was innocently excited about it. I explained how helpful it had been, how we had used the information, and how it had helped Toni, too, in understanding herself. She acted as if I had gotten Dr. Federici out of a Cracker Jack box. I tried to explain his 30-page credentials, his nationally-recognized efforts, and the fact that he had seen over 12,000 children. I tried to explain that I planned to go to someone local, but I decided to save up to go to an expert in the field as we needed someone who understood and could help us. It was to no avail.

I was accused of selecting a neuropsychologist who I could manipulate. She began by asking if our plan was to have Toni to go into the military. I answered in the affirmative except that it was Toni's idea, not ours. She went on to say that if she had a mental illness, she would not be able to go into the military and that is why we had her tested. I said it was true that if there was an underlying mental illness, she should not join the military or it would exacerbate it, and we wanted to be sure she could continue on her chosen path safely, as well as other benefits an evaluation provides the parents and child. I was accused of telling Dr. Federici what to write in the evaluation so that we could force Toni go into the military. My mouth dropped. How can you untwist someone so twisted?

I realized that Toni had fed her these lies and the county case worker had called her ahead of time. All I could do is reiterate everything that I said about it being her future plan to join the military and that we cannot force her to do anything. I certainly did not have the power to force a nationally-known neuropsychologist to lie in his evaluation for our benefit. Her accusations were ridiculous, and could not be farther from the truth.

After digesting all of my meetings thus far, I came to a realization. We needed to hire an attorney to represent us. I believed it was God telling me what we needed to do because it came to me suddenly and it was more like a statement than a thought in my mind that maybe we ought to do that. I knew we had to and I knew who to get. Most of the time, James and I discuss things, especially if it involves spending our money or important issues. I know he works hard for his money, and I believe in being careful with it. When we splurge on things, I feel he should be involved so I rarely, if ever, eat out without him or go on a shopping spree, except for groceries and necessities. When I attempted to address the issue with James, he said it before I did. I knew that was the confirmation we needed, and James called her right away. The attorney knew us personally, so she felt terrible for our situation. She also knew how the system worked and knew how they can railroad someone and not feel badly. We knew that we would make a good trophy should the county finally get us founded and on the list of child abusers.

We Know You, AND We Love You

I was worried that Jadin did not understand Toni's motives or the desperate measures she would take to get her motives accomplished, but he thought he did. I love Jadin and his wife, and our grandchild dearly and I did not want to see them get hurt. When I expressed my fears, he said, "She is not going to jeopardize my job!" He said it as if we allowed it to happen to us and there were warning signs. Toni is subtle and conniving, and much of the time we thought everything was going well. We also warned him that she will manipulate and get people in trouble by taking medications she is not supposed to take, but he did not lock his medications up. We told him she will do whatever it takes to be alone with a guy as her main objective was to get pregnant at sixteen, but he allowed her to date. We told him she will secretly hurt their child, but he had her babysit him often. I know, at one point, his son burned his hand with Toni's electric hair straightener. We did not believe it was an accident, and Jadin began to wonder if it was on purpose. I prayed often for their safety and besides being angered and annoyed at her ungratefulness, sloppiness, disrespect and lies, they came out of their good deed relatively unscathed. Their computer did not survive long after Toni was told she had to cut down on how much she spent on social media. The computer was "accidentally" left on the trunk of the car by Toni just before they were driving away out a store parking lot and was never seen again.

We remained her parents from afar while she lived with Jadin and his family. We contacted her often, talking to her on the phone and visiting her. Our family had found an excellent holistic nutritionist and chiropractor that I wanted her to see. So one day, I got someone to watch the younger children and drove two hours to get Toni, drove more than an hour to get to the doctors' office, and then returned her. I bought her herbs that help pain during PMS and she loved them. I kept her supplied.

They seemed to help her and I wanted to once again, show her how much I cared about her and her needs. I wanted to show her that parents take care of their children, as they transition into adulthood. During our ride to and from the doctor's office, we had plenty of time to talk. She babbled on and on about other people and what they were doing wrong in life. She gossiped about Jadin and his wife and what neglectful parents they were. She gossiped about my son's friend and how she saw on his cell phone on multiple occasions that he was texting another woman, even though he was married. She had plenty to say until I asked her if she had made that list yet, that I asked her to make.

I wanted her to write down all that she had in our home, all the good things that she willingly left because she could not wait eight more months until she finished her college classes and turned seventeen. She admitted that she had not written anything down yet, so I took that opportunity to once again use the reality therapy I learned. I explained to her that she has a destructive pattern of hurting people and destroying her life and her future every time things are going well in her life. I verbally listed a few examples such as a paid job, college classes and that people like her bosses adored her. I pointed out to her that she does not allow herself to be happy, content and calm and that she thrives on chaos and destroyed relationships. This is why I wanted her to write things down for her to see in black and white. She remained quiet and had nothing more to say. I guess it was a conversation-ender for someone who had no intention of changing or doing well in life.

After a while of awkward silence, I switched topics and asked her about her shopping trip with Brittani. She brightened up and proudly told me that Brittani took her shopping. All the while, her new husband stood by astounded at how much she was spending on her credit card to get Toni new clothes, some of which she said she did not need or want. Brittani's husband tried to speak up, but Brittani shot him a death look that shut him up for the remainder of the agonizing shopping trip. She laughingly explained that Brittani is in total control of that household. Toni exclaimed that Brittani spent over a thousand dollars on her. I was happy to hear that Toni was so blessed, even though she had bags and bags and boxes and boxes of clothes at Jadin's house, including some new clothes with the tags still on them.

I asked her if Brittani knew that she was talking to James and I, visiting with us and hanging out with us. She said, "No, I have not told her." I said, "Good. It is good to keep it a secret because then you can get more out of Brittani." Toni gave me a look of amazement, as if to say, "You know how I operate." I smiled. I said, "Yeah, if Brittani knew you were getting along fine with us, she would not be buying you things. And meanwhile, you get what you need from us too." I looked straight ahead and quietly drove her back to Jadin's house.

On that trip to the nutritionist and chiropractor, I was blessed to have my grandson with me. I enjoyed getting to know him more, even though he was only two years old. We missed his two-year-old birthday party, as Toni was living there and had alleged that we had abused her on her way out of our home, so we could not put our family in jeopardy by being around her. She gloated at the fact that we could not attend our grandson's birthday party. It broke my heart, and there was nothing we could do. Our children's safety was our main concern. Taking her to this doctor visit was risky enough.

The Snowball Effect

Our next meeting with the caseworkers was in the lawyer's office. Our children sat in the waiting room where the social worker said "hello" to each of them, noticing their genuine smiles and happiness. During the meeting, I educated the young, childless caseworker about traumatized children, their tendencies, and their outlooks on life. I also explained how I have learned from experts such as Heather Forbes and Dr. Ronald Federici to deal properly with a traumatized child, without using control, consequences or logic, as these simply do not work. I was able to address a letter the previous caseworkers had sent me regarding appropriate discipline. It was a ridiculous letter. In the letter, the caseworker and her supervisor informed James and me that they were "completing an investigation that was made to the State Central Registry." They went on to advise us that "taking away something that is meaningful, such as TV time, or a game may prove to be effective and giving the children a 'time-out' and making them sit in that time out for perhaps 5 minutes may also be successful." The letter ended with what James and I perceived as a threat, stating that "if a report is received at our department regarding excessive corporal punishment, family court action may be taken."

Traumatized children should be put in a Time-In situation because being with an adult helps them regulate their stress level, as opposed to being rejected and placed in Time-Out in a room, corner or chair. Taking away a game from children who faced starvation as young children was not a punishment, they were familiar with being denied things they wanted and needed. Besides, our children do not have the typical cell phones and electronic game systems their peers have. We enjoy Monopoly, Yahtzee and Sequence. It made no sense to take our family games from them. Traumatized children should be encouraged to be included, not excluded.

I addressed each 'machine gunned' question that the child protective workers had asked the other day. I had a captive audience and a lawyer to stop me if I was saying too much. One of the issues with me was that we were working through a workbook, Surviving Sexual Abuse. Thinking that it would show that we were attempting to help Toni and our other children through their trauma and abuses, it was foreign to me that they would have such a problem with it. I was confused but able to explain further that many of these children were sexually abused somewhere in their transitions in their traumatic lives, but I had chosen that book because Dr. Federici had suggested it. He said that it would address topics that a traumatized child would benefit from, not just a sexually-abused individual. He said the majority of the book could be used for all of the children if I paraphrased and taught them each lesson. We incorporated it into our classes and meetings at home.

I was in control of that meeting, taking the opportunity to lecture the uneducated caseworker. I relished the opportunity to help her understand the traumatized child. I got excited about advocating for these children. After the meeting, I sheepishly asked the lawyer if the meeting went alright, or if I had made a grave mistake. She said she was impressed and that the meeting went well.

My husband and I were adamant that we wanted Toni re-evaluated. We wanted the focus back onto her destructive patterns, her behavioral issues and her tendency to create her own reality. Dr. Federici insisted that it was PTSD (post-traumatic stress disorder) that was driving her poor decisions and angry actions, but we felt that a more recent evaluation might uncover something or put a light on her more recent issues for the judge and social workers. We filed a court petition against Toni in hopes to take the attention off of us, and back onto the troubled child where it belonged. It did put attention onto her, but it certainly did not take it off of us. The petition saved us though, as well as having a paper trail of documents. Two years later, our friends had a similar situation where their troubled child ran away. They feared for their family's safety and refused to allow her back into their home, but insisted on placement for the child. They did not timely file a petition against their child. Their dream was to have their daughter get the help she needed, but knowing our experience, knew that it would probably not happen. Our friends were arrested for refusing to take their dangerous child back into the home. We, thankfully, never got that far in our struggles with our children.

We hoped for sustainable healing and contentment. We were asked to meet with the psychologist chosen by the county for Toni's evaluation. We did not realize how intimate the county/psychologist relationship was. We were open and forthright with her. She seemed to listen. We explained that Toni obviously has some problems and is begging for help. We explained that we had found a note of an unknown date stating that she took an array of pills. Furthermore, we noted that we did not know if it was true and we never noticed her being ill or in danger. We explained that we took precautionary steps to ensure her safety, such as locking up all meds in the house.

A week or so after our meeting with the psychologist, child protective workers were again at our door. We were being accused of "Not getting our daughter help." I laughed at the two workers because the allegations were absurd. I was in the middle of preparing my sermon for my mother's burial that afternoon. If you do not believe in evil or Satan, this would be a prime example in my opinion. I sat down in the old-fashioned rocking chair on my side porch and smiled at the two young informers. I mockingly asked if the next workers were going to tell me she had too much ear wax in her ear. With a case already open, I was not sure why they felt they had to open a whole new case for this. I explained that we were the only ones concerned with Toni's needs and issues and that the whole point of meeting with the psychologist that made these allegations was to get Toni help. I had also explained that we had recently spent thousands of dollars to get her tested by a nationally-known expert who in turn gave us several suggestions on how to approach her individualized needs. Amazingly, we were reported to the child abuse hotline for not getting our daughter help by the same professional we had been referred to as part of the petition against our daughter. It did not make sense.

I then explained that the psychiatrist, child protective workers and domestic violence workers should be accused of not caring about my daughter's needs and not getting her help. No one brought her to an emergency room though she claimed to have been slammed against a wall several times. Could not that cause a concussion or some type of major problem? No one will ensure that the medications in her new placement are locked up. No one will get her counseling or therapy. The child protective workers left my porch with an understanding air about them, but the investigation into these baseless allegations remained open for the maximum allowable time.

The petition against our child in this case was helpful. Family court is never fun, even if you are the good guy. We have learned from the past to have a lawyer to speak for us as the courtroom can become chaotic and words can be misconstrued. Jadin and his wife, as well as Dedra, Dedra's friend, Brittani and her new husband, appeared for the initial hearing. This was the first time we had seen Brittani and her husband since they got married. He remains silent and is rather nonexistent. Interestingly, Brittani looked to us in the lobby for support, reassurance and understanding, and used our lawyer to draw up legal papers for her after the hearing. The common cause seemed to unite us for a few short hours.

Toni busily played all sides while Dedra and her friend spoke loudly about us, mocking us in an attempt to anger us in some way. Dedra and her friend had called us several times in the weeks leading up to the hearing to demand 17% of our gross income as child support for Toni.

I prayed that this time together would prove to Brittani we have nothing against her and that we still love her despite how she has treated us, but that would not be the case. When the judge announced her decision, Dedra's friend skirted quickly out of the courtroom. She took Toni by the hand and ran out of the lobby and dodged the county sheriffs. Toni eventually turned herself into the police three months later.

After the court hearing, Brittani and her husband had lunch beside us at a fast food place while the judge decided what to do about

Toni fleeing. Police could not locate them that day, so we were all asked to come in the next morning to fill out paperwork. The next morning, Brittani had regrouped and realigned herself with her fabricated reality and was meaner than ever. She did not look at us or speak to us with respect. It was as if we were not there. The court security guards whom we had befriended by now were confused at the difference they were seeing in her. We just shrugged our shoulders. We did not want to change who we were because she decided to change. We are who we are and we love her despite her cruelty toward us. We do not view adoption as temporary. We are not perfect, but feel perfectly suited for each of our children.

Worlds Collide

At the end of this trying year, we decided to visit James's best friend more than a thousand miles away in Arizona. His college friend was not feeling well and seemed to need a friend. With lodging taken care of by his best friend, we basically just needed to get there and buy food for our days there. As I thought about the year we had and how difficult it was on all of us, I wanted to do something to help seal our family bond and give us some much needed relaxation and fun. I began exploring the idea of a trip to Disneyland. It would take the place of Christmas presents, but I felt that it would be worth the sacrifice. I figured we could also get them all a sweatshirt from the Disneyland store on our way out. And so we planned a two-day visit to Disneyland.

Our trip was everything we needed and wanted it to be. There was a small part of me that was sad for Toni. She never made it to any Disney theme park because of her behavior problems. The last time we planned to take Toni, Chloe and Brittani to Disney in Florida, we had to go home prematurely because of their disrespect, screaming fits and embarrassing attitude problems. They never knew all that we had planned. We could not go through with it.

However, this trip was outstanding. We had never had children that could have fun without having an attitude about anything and everything. We enjoyed each other and laughed a lot. Our trip to Disney was an amazing blessing. We went on the busiest day of the year, but were still able to do everything we wanted to do and get on every ride we wanted to get on. We spent two days from 6 am wake up time to 11 pm bedtime with no attitudes except for Rebekka having a problem finding the right sweatshirt she wanted the second day.

The trip was beyond our budget, but we assumed we would have time to pay it off soon enough. We had no idea how quickly and drastically things would change for us. Both James and I felt drawn to move to Phoenix, Arizona. We felt it was time to live in Arizona where my husband had always dreamed of living. I had to point to God for me to feel that way. I never had the desire to move, let alone move to Arizona due to its extremely hot climate. My health condition made it more dangerous for me to live in the desert. I searched for God's Will. It scared me to think that we were to leave everything we had ever known and our dream house to live so far away.

Three weeks after returning from Arizona, the kids and I traveled 12 hours to visit a good friend, Peggy, who also had adopted children from my children's orphanage. We had met at an adoption reunion. Again, I had felt drawn to this reunion, as if I was meant to be there, regardless of how far away it was or that I had to do it alone with our three African children at the time: Rebekka, Josh and Samuel. I wanted our internationally-adopted children to feel a part of something so much bigger and perhaps connect with other children from the same orphanage, and they did. We befriended Peggy and her family and have served as reliable support systems for one another.

While visiting Peggy, her Christian friend came to visit. We got talking and she said she had a Word from the Lord for me, that we were "going to move soon and that God would bless us with a better house than we already have." Peggy's friend did not know me, nor did she know I lived in what I considered my dream home, nor did she know my husband and I were contemplating moving. I had only met her once before. I broke into tears at the thought that God heard my need to have our move confirmed and heard my sad heart reinvigorated by the prospects of a possible move.

Not long after that, James went up for prayer by an evangelist at church, and he also confirmed, without knowing anything about us or our situation, that he would be "traveling by commuter train to work and back." Meanwhile, I got a prophecy from his wife that, although I have "felt worried and felt that what I have done in my life, has not been

212

worthwhile, God sees what I have done and our children are like flowers before me in a large bouquet." Prophecies such as these are not necessary in a Christian's life and many people scoff at such a thing, but prophecy can bring confirmation, encouragement and strength to a questioning Christian. A Christian also must be careful and test the Spirit, as not all those with prophetic words are from God. We must put the prophecy against Scripture because Scripture always prevails. Prophecy also never conjures up the dead or speaks to the dead.

Not Again

Before James and I got serious about moving and making plans, Rebekka began experiencing an aftershock of sorts. After the rough year with Toni leaving and constant scrutiny by child protective services, perhaps the overstimulation of the Disney theme park and the thought of moving from everything that was familiar to her was too much.

Rebekka began having small fits of rage like she had infrequently when she was younger. Her first small fit was at Disneyland when she could not find a sweatshirt she wanted to buy. Her fits begin with her acting like a statue – she refuses to eat, drink, go anywhere, or do anything. Her body and brain shut down. Her demeanor changes and her eyes become sunken in, dark and beady. Interestingly, her breath would begin to smell like she ate a dead animal. She would not respond to anything we would say or do, until she acted out/exploded. These fits always ended badly with running away and violence. Sometimes, we could hold her down as a family and pray over her, singing Christian songs, speaking softly to her about how much we cared about her and loved her, until her rage subsided three to four hours later. Someone inevitably got kicked hard in the stomach or an arm twisted or bitten. She would throw up, spit, make growling noises and bang her head on the floor.

Once these fits started to reoccur, it was an unending nightmare. I was disappointed because she had not had a fit in years and I thought we had gotten past that part of her traumatized life and trauma response. I thought she had bonded and loved us more than this. I used reality therapy to explain all of this to her, that once a habit begins (going into fits of rage rather than communicating effectively), it would be that much more difficult to end. I begged her not to go that direction, but she did. I felt sad for her that she felt she had to resort to this response. It seemed that every time she entered into this trauma response, she killed brain cells. I have no proof that this happens, but for example, before she began these fits, she could cook us a well-balanced meal. After a year of these fits, she could no longer cook anything without supervision because she would do something incorrectly or sometimes even dangerous – she regressed terribly.

The year is now a blur in some ways, but it was tumultuous and chaotic. I knew that it was heart trouble with Rebekka, but there was no getting through to her. She spent a year being angry, disrespectful, mean and spiteful. Our year was spent trying to do enough and say enough to let her know how much we loved her and that we were her family, willing to stick with her as we always have.

After a fit of rage, where Rebekka banged her head against the wall and floor, she became increasingly more agitated. If we let her have her space, she got worse. If I stayed with her or nearby, she got worse. She began to destroy the house and kick the children's toys while they were playing with them. She would pace back and forth angrily, so much so on one occasion that a responding police officer was nervous and called for backup. On another occasion, she grabbed a kitchen knife and ran out of the house. I was unsure whether to follow her. To give her attention might worsen it, whereas letting her go, might not give her the attention she craved. To not follow her, would show her that I did not care, and if anything happened, how would I explain to authorities why I did not try to stop her?

I knew there was no good answer for what to do – you do not think of how to respond to your child running around wielding a knife ahead of time. I followed her and talked to her from a safe distance. She continued to scrape the knife softly across her skin on her arm. None of our knives were sharp enough to do any damage with this motion. I did not feel like she would do anything, but I also knew that she had so much rage inside of her, she might do something rash. I called the crisis line and her counselor. They did not feel that anything needed to be done. I called them each several times and begged them to pay attention to Rebekka's cries for help, before she resorted to something more drastic.

Rebekka's first psychiatric hospital stay was in April of that year. Rebekka had continued having outbursts, but the reason for the fits were less founded in reality. She used to have fits when she felt blamed for doing something wrong, including when she was caught red-handed. Now, we had no idea what was going to set her off.

After struggling to get through to her, I used a new approach when she had her next outburst. I tried to be near her to let her know that I cared and that I would not give up on her. I was not overbearing or in her face, but remained in the general area of her room. As her agitation worsened, I attempted to talk calmly to her. As she grew worse, I quietly told the kids to call the police. While the police were being called, she nailed me with an upper cut to the face, giving me a concussion. Fortunately, Josh came to my rescue and kept her from hitting me again. Rebekka viciously bit his arm during the altercation. Eventually the police arrived and whisked her off to the nearby emergency room.

I was proud of Josh for protecting me. He felt that pain for several months, and he still has the scar to fuel his bitterness for her. There was such a peace in our home when Rebekka was in the psychiatric facility. Meanwhile, however, I was criticized by the emergency room social workers and the psychiatric hospital staff. Rebekka's attack on Josh was ignored by every professional.

Rebekka spent most of her year in and out of psychiatric hospitals. Each time the hospital prepared for discharge, they refused to address her attitude and the root cause of her outbursts, and there was never any discussion, advice or tips for dealing with PTSD. I knew hospital stays would make her worse, i.e. adopting the behaviors of the other patients and the insecurity of being rejected again, but to have her home became more and more dangerous, no matter what we tried. The psychiatric hospital she kept returning to, did not listen to us, did not include us in her care, and kept disregarding her needs. Interestingly, we were suddenly more credible after she beat up staff and had to be tranquilized to calm down, but they continued to ignore her issues and planned for her discharge two days later. They blamed the other girl for instigating her.

The last hospital she went into was a privately-run hospital. They did not keep her as long as the state-run hospital, but they allowed me to be involved in her treatment and counseling. I was able to sit for a couple hours in her room with her, talking to her. I ate dinner with her and participated in family therapy that evening.

This hospital realized the role parents play in their children's mental health treatment, and in six days they did what the other hospital could not do in four months. Consequently, Rebekka missed out on family activities and special trips. I sent cards nearly every day expressing my love and concern for her and encouraging her to open up to them so that she could break the cycle of despair. I visited her often, only to endure her cold silence. Upon her return, she reported that she felt abandoned and did not think we cared about her because one of the girls at the psychiatric hospital told her we did not care. Rebekka gained more than seventy pounds in this year of inactivity that has been impossible for her to lose.

During this year of psychiatric stays for Rebekka, we had been bombarded with abuse allegations. They had dragged on from the previous year and lasted almost the entire following year. We felt powerless as allegation after allegation was left open for investigation well after the allotted 60 day time period. I cannot relay how difficult it is to parent challenging children while being watched continuously. They were just waiting for us to slip up in some way. In the meantime, James and I knew we had to escape this oppression. We spent most of our days cleaning, organizing, packing, giving things away and having a large garage sale. Originally we had planned to pack a U-Haul but after months of packing boxes, we realized we did not have the money to transport our belongings. All of our beds were at least 10 years old, so we could not see the point in transporting them. I began unpacking boxes and separating the most important items for the purpose of keeping them. We tried to keep it at a bare minimum as my eight passenger vehicle would have little room for our belongings and James' car was only a medium sized four door sedan.

The day we received the letter stating we were cleared from all abuse charges from the last open case, the kids and I left. My vehicle had been packed for several days waiting for this opportunity to leave. James

217

wanted me to leave that evening but I insisted that I was exhausted and needed a good night's sleep. Usually, this role is reversed, but I think the stress of it all had exhausted me.

I left the next morning at 5 am with Rebekka, Josh, Anna, Samuel, Dawson, our family dog and as many belongings we could fit in the vehicle. I felt like a refugee. The trip was not easy, but surprisingly, I made good time. I was awake and alert, with fear and apprehension of what lay ahead. I was also excited and anxious to start our new life. I was scared and lonely because I left my most precious belonging behind: my husband.

Phoenix - The Beginning of Healing

Driving up to the house, I recognize it immediately from the pictures on the internet. I recognize it as if it was meant to be mine. I am nervous. I am lonely. I do not know anything about setting up a home - gas, water, utilities, garbage, air conditioning, electricity. I have not moved in fifteen years and planned to remain in our country Victorian home forever. I cannot look back; I have to look forward. I have a lot to do, but my main goal is to facilitate healing for all of us.

I now drive up to our humble, single-story 80's style, 4 bedrooms, 2300 square-foot, stucco tract home, I breathe deeply and smile. We sacrificed everything in order to pursue the peace and contentment needed for our family to flourish. Now I had that peace, contentment, joy, freedom- and my family!

As a Phoenix rises from the ashes, we, too, are arising from the ashes – our trials and tribulations of life. We are Phoenix Bound!

MoVeing to AZ

I Was Scard When
We moVed I didn't know
What to expect. I Was Scard
of duststorms, drouts, and rattelsnak
but know I love AraZona.

Epilogue

I wrote this book to help people become more aware of the realities of adoption and how others' uneducated and inexperienced opinions and comments can impact a vulnerable family. This book is a glimpse of that reality, based on our reality. This is not everyone's reality nor is it inevitably going to happen if you choose to adopt, but many of the struggles and heart issues may be the same. My greatest fear is to discourage people that are meant to adopt from adoption, but I do feel that the truth needs to be out there: a truth that could become a reality for you. Adoption is either glorified by TV, movies, books and our compassionate hearts, or it is seen by people as second best. It is neither. It is simply a chosen way to form a family, but it does come with some difficulties and/or challenges that people need to be aware of. Sometimes the fear of the unknown is worse than the knowing. It is much easier to deal with problems that arise in life, if we are prepared and understand what is going on. In adoption, many adoptive parents, the adoptees themselves and the birth parents are left dealing with their emotions alone, thinking that they are going crazy. Sometimes, knowing that their emotions and thoughts are normal can do a world of good for all involved. Knowing the root cause can create an avenue for healing for the adoptee as well as the adoptive parents.

My husband and I are not saints for adopting, nor are we crazy, nor are we the horrible parents that some people have pegged us to be. We are probably somewhere in the middle of all that. We are somewhat ordinary parents that put their all into parenting children that did not have a family that could take on their needs. Our greatest fault is trying too hard and refusing to give up on our children. We are dedicated and committed to each other and to each of our children whether they reciprocate that or not. We are continuously trying to improve our parenting skills based on our children's needs and issues. We have taken on a challenge that many people respectfully shy away from. We were called to do this work and do not regret the difficulties and struggles that we have been through while pursuing this mission. At times, I am jealous and covet the normal family. I look longingly at their large family photo with all of their children in attendance, smiling, all wearing white shirts and standing close, knowing that it would take a miracle for us to have the same.

Adoptive parents need to always think ahead and be aware of adoptive issues in nearly all facets of life. For example, our children need their own rooms. Resorting back to orphanage or foster care behaviors, such as hoarding food and acting out sexually, comes naturally to them when stressed, which can be triggered by the smallest of things. It can be understood when you think of a death in your family or a tragedy. Something as small as a smell or a sound can bring it all back and send through your brain and body, an overwhelming feeling of loss and sadness. These children live this on a daily basis and often resort to old behaviors.

My prayer is that you will glean from my book what you will need to prepare yourself for the realities of adoption, commiserate and feel a bond with us, or understand what adoptive parents go through, or perhaps you are an adoptee and you needed to hear from an adoptive mother's heart, the love that you never felt. It was almost impossible to give you a picture of our daily struggle, but I summarized and gave you a broader perspective of the struggles we have faced as adoptive parents. Adoption can crush a human spirit or it can revive it; it depends on the outlook and perception of everyone involved. My husband and I are made for adopting. Ideally, we do not regret any of our adoptions and we do not expect more from our children than they can deliver. There are days when we focus too much on how much we wanted for our children, but we have to be content at where they are. Adopting children is our life's work and we will adopt until the Lord says our "quiver is full," not when someone tells us we have too many children.

It was difficult to re-live our life in order to put it down on paper. It was difficult for my husband to read and for me to re-read. I hope it was a worthwhile endeavor. Our openness contributes to our healing process and it will continue to work within us. The individuals in the adoptive triad are misled and have unrealistic expectations. They are left without support and are often hurting inside. The pain they feel comes out in many ways when it cannot be expressed appropriately with people who understand. I also urge adoptive parents to befriend the birth parent where it is possible to do so and to listen to their child's heart. Our children's behaviors are coming from deep within. Many of our older children have built such a stone wall around their heart that we could only poke occasional holes into it, only to be filled with an even stronger epoxy. In our case, the people in our surroundings helped our children fill these holes with the stronger epoxy.

Our struggles might lend a conspirator's hand to the old legend that these kids are bad blood or that all adoptive children are bad, but it is not true. Our struggles reflect our children's struggles in their hearts and minds. Left to themselves, our children will compound their pain. We all do that to some extent. We all have made things immensely worse than they really were, either by worrying or negative self-talk or dwelling on a portion of our circumstance. However, adoptive children, are not 'typical' in the sense that they began their lives with loss and rejection and will live with that for the remainder of their days.

Adoption is not a bad choice for parents that cannot parent them, nor is adoption a bad thing for the child or the adoptive parents. I am a strong supporter of adoption and always will be, but prospective adoptive parents need to stop diving into adoption with a mindset that they are filling gaps in their lives or that they are "saving the child's life." Although these may be true, it clashes with the realities and harshness of adoption. Adoptive parents need to be willing to learn and understand their child's struggles and the source of the behaviors they will see. My dream for our children was that they would recognize and strive to emulate the strength and fortitude that James and I have tried desperately to portray for them through our difficult times.

Dr. Federici recently visited us, evaluating most of our children for the second time and evaluating our youngest two for the first time.

223

He was relieved to know that we had moved out of the county and state that was harassing us. He said that when they questioned him about us, they treated him like he was lower than them, discounting and arguing with what he said. How can a caseworker in a small county from a community college have the authority to discredit and disallow any credence of a seasoned neuropsychologist, who is an adoption expert, and often used as an expert witness in courts throughout the United States? How can they not respect the position he holds as an expert in his field? Dr. Federici has served hundreds of times as an expert in court proceedings and seen more than 12,000 children in his private practice. He has traveled extensively and is well-respected in other countries. He has earned his doctorate degree, researched extensively and written books. He can provide over 30 pages of credentials. How many pages of accomplishments and credentials can this un-intimidated case worker provide? He has also adopted several children from orphanages. Unfortunately, these helping professions generally do not pay well, which attracts people who are using their job as either a stepping stone or a dead end in their lives due to their lack of education or lack of ability to get a better paying job.

Dr. Federici's evaluations showed a marked increase of trauma for each child, since he had last seen them, only months before the chaos and abuse allegations began. His evaluations showed that our children had gone down in IQ and EQ due to the extra trauma and stress they had experienced in the last three years before moving to Arizona. Anna uses 'Anna Land' more frequently, allowing her to hide within herself and has more anxiety and depression. In Dr. Federici's evaluation session with each of our children, they spoke of insecurities and fears relating to the caseworkers' interrogations and intimidation methods. As much as I tried to protect my children from the harmful effects of the baseless child protective investigations, I could not. They were like wolves surrounding us – getting ready for a kill. Dr. Federici also insisted that Rebekka does not have a mental illness and should never have been hospitalized. He adamantly stated that the stress, insecurities and post-traumatic stress disorder caused her outbursts and confusion. As atrocious as Rebekka's behaviors were, her greatest fear was that we would give up on her. Without the ability to process and communicate her emotions, she lashed out. It pains me to think that she spent most of a year in a psychiatric hospital, destroyed two years of her life, and is taking four medications now, due to an insensitive harassment of the child protective system. If we had gotten the support we needed, rather than the harassment we received, would she have been able to bypass the psychiatric stays and medication regime? Will Brittani, Chloe, and Toni ever care about what they did to their younger siblings' hearts and minds? Had the therapist understood the situation and addressed it appropriately, would Rebekka have been able to communicate her feelings and process them? Rebekka's main focus of moving was losing her best friend whom she had not seen in several years. Perhaps someone could have come alongside us and helped her through that pain of rejection for years and the pain of losing her forever. Perhaps someone could have redirected her to her family who loves her?

Without Dr. Federici involved in our older children's lives, we will never know the inner workings of Miguel and Jesslyn, but I am wondering if it is not similar or identical. If child protective services had supported us and helped us work through Jesslyn's post-traumatic stress response to her frightening visions, would she have been able to remain in our home and enjoy a normal childhood? If so, would Miguel have remained the fun, happy-go-lucky child he was without the insecurities of the child protective services? If the former foster parent or in-laws in Brittani's situation had used reality to combat her anger and bitterness, would she have come back to us in tears and humility? If her husband had refused to marry a bitter and angry young lady, would she have been forced to deal with her true feelings rather than use us as her scapegoat? Thinking about the possibilities of a supportive system and the possibilities of my children being protected from further trauma invigorates me to write my story. Professionals should also take into consideration that, by the time they get involved, the adoptive parents are overwhelmed with anger and frustration and the child feels lost, confused and angry. These questions haunt me on a regular basis. James and I wanted so much for our children. We wanted them to know and enjoy a normal childhood, feeling loved, safe and secure, despite their obvious adoptive status.

In my attempt to help our children feel secure and safe, we held family meetings, discussed their feelings regularly, played therapeutic board games, detailed this trauma in their adoption journey book, read trauma books together and cuddled with them. Dawson still talks about the inappropriate questions the case workers asked, his shame of lying to them, and the fear the caseworkers invoked. His comment at age seven sums it up as he asked confused one day, "Aren't those people (case workers) supposed to help us, not hurt us?"

During lunch one day, Dawson remembered the time we were in a large crosswalk outside a local museum, when we saw a car approaching. There were six of us and we were well seen in the daylight, but the car seemed to speed up. As the kids and I hurried across, we looked into the eyes of the driver and each child recognized her to be a caseworker once on our case. I agreed it looked like her and it seemed she purposefully sped up, but I did not want our kids to be more traumatized than they already were. I sheepishly disagreed with them and reassured them that the driver would have slowed down if needed. This happened in the same city the caseworker's offices were in. Other times, I remember a car sitting at the bottom of our hill for a long period of time and the kids using binoculars to see who it was, convinced that it was a case worker. I would explain that many times when someone has a phone call to make, they will pull over where it was safe to do so. Despite the bad memories, I am relieved and content that we are now living in an environment of peace and healing that our children can feel safe in. We have never been happier. The effects of the trauma caused a myriad of aftershock effects in Arizona, but the peace and contentment underlies it all. It was also worth losing everything we had. We could not put a price on peace and liberty.

Five months after the kids and I moved to Arizona, James was able to join us. He accepted a job in Phoenix and was able to give his two-week notice at his old job. We were once again a family; a traumatized family, rising from the ashes of condemnation, oppression and persecution.

I have changed names of people and places involved to keep their privacy.

Never the End

Angie K Elliston

My husband and I have adopted from the foster care system, adoption disruptions, internationally, and privately. Our oldest at adoption placement was 16 years old and our youngest was a newborn. We have seen trauma 'up close and personal'. PHOENIX BOUND is an honest, heart-felt story that explores how we navigated through the obstacles and trials of raising 13 children, society's expectations, and our eventual rise from the ashes of destruction to start a new life.

www.phoenixboundbook.com

PhoenixBoundQuest@gmail.com

Angie is also a co-author of Best-seller, EMPOWERING WOMEN TO SUCCEED: Turning Tragedy Into Triumph where she shares her personal story before she began adopting.

The book encourages and inspires women to have faith in healing from their past, starting over and overcoming challenges in order to fulfill their destiny. It is powerful, engaging, and inspirational. A must read for all. It reveals how successful women have faced huge, life-changing transitions in the areas of health, divorce, loss of loved ones, wealth and much more. Their stories will inspire you to step out of toxic relationships, heal from abuse and shame, and start living a joyous life. You may have been bruised in life, but nothing can break your spirit. You are in charge of creating the life of your dreams and surrounding yourself with healthy people who truly love, support, and celebrate you. This book will provide you with the courage and strength to overcome any situation, forgive those who have harmed you and turn your tragedy into triumph. The key message is about how a woman's mindset determines her outcome in life, business and relationships.

Made in the USA
Las Vegas, NV
12 November 2022

59314484R00133